Outside the Bungalow

OUTSIDE THE BUNGALOW
America's Arts & Crafts Garden

PAUL DUCHSCHERER
PHOTOGRAPHS BY DOUGLAS KEISTER

PENGUIN STUDIO

**This book is dedicated to the generous spirit of the homeowners
who shared their gardens with us,
and to those pursuits of pleasure, inspiration, and magic
that only a garden can provide.**

Raised corner spa of a bungalow in Marin County, California. Deciding on the placement of this spa was easy, for the only space it could fit into was in this rear corner. Although most of the limited open space was designed as a paved patio area for outdoor entertaining, the owner wanted to retain the feeling of a garden and preserve some room for plantings. The idea of raising the spa avoided excavation, and the short run of stairs required to reach it act as a partial screen, while providing extra casual seating if needed. The height of the fence at the far side provides needed privacy, but its bulk is reduced by a running lattice-filled window in its upper portion. Permitting more light and interwoven with climbing roses, an all-lattice top is used on the fence across the back of the property at left. A unique detail at its top uses lengths of copper piping to form the cross-bars of a pergola-like projection designed to support flowering vines. An extension of the fence treatment is used to screen the spa from the kitchen or the street. Set amid lush plantings, a cast-iron fountain is tucked into a corner at the right. Handmade ceramic-tile accents add interest to the brick paving. (For other views of this house see figs. 77, 248-250, 267; also *Inside the Bungalow*, illustration opposite page 1, figs. 69, 89, 110, 120, 121.)

PENGUIN STUDIO
Published by the Penguin Group
Penguin Putnam Inc., 375 Hudson Street,
New York, New York 10014, U.S.A.

Penguin Books Ltd, 27 Wrights Lane,
London W8 5TZ, England

Penguin Books Australia Ltd, Ringwood,
Victoria, Australia

Penguin Books Canada Ltd, 10 Alcorn Avenue,
Toronto, Ontario, Canada M4V 3B2

Penguin Books (N.Z.) Ltd, 182-90 Wairau Road,
Auckland 10, New Zealand

Penguin Books Ltd, Registered Offices:
Harmondsworth, Middlesex, England

First published in the United States by Penguin Studio,
a member of Penguin Putnam Inc.

First Printing, August 1999

10 9 8 7 6 5 4 3 2 1

Copyright © Paul Duchscherer and Douglas Keister 1999
All rights reserved.

Library of Congress Catalog Card Number: 99-70250

Book designed by Marilyn Rey
Printed and bound by Dai Nippon Printing Co., Hong Kong, Ltd.

ISBN: 0-670-88355-7

CONTENTS

ACKNOWLEDGMENTS

We wish to extend our deepest gratitude, appreciation, and thanks to the following homeowners, whose generosity in sharing their personal environments has made this book possible: Linda and Paul Addison, Louis J. Bader house homeowners, Jane Brackman and Rod Holcomb, Marilyn and George Brumder, Catharine and Gerard Brown / Floating World Wood Design, Noel Angell and Emory Bundy, Debbie and Louis Beacham / Beacham Construction Inc., David E. Berman / Trustworth Studios / Sconehenge, Ann Boynton, George Campbell and Terrence O'Shea, Ellen Casey, Charlene Casey, Helen and Robson Chambers, Katherine Chapman-Ord and Kent Ord, Ann and Andre Chaves, Bruce Chevillat, Karen and Don Covington, Dawn-Starr Crowther and David Eshbaugh, Cathie and Bill Daniels, Edna and Charles Davidson, Lynne and Audel Davis, Louis F. D'Elia, James Ellis and Roger Deakins, Gloria and Leon De Leon, Olivia Dresher, Jana and Steve Drobinsky / Omega Too, Marguerite Duncan-Abrams and Michael Abrams, Lauren Gabor and Scott D. Goldstein, Judith Geist, Claudia Geletka and Rob Winovich, Evelyn and Gary Glenn, Foster Goldstrom, Lauren Rickey Greene, David Greene, Tina Panella-Hart and James Hart, Ingrid Helton and Erik Hanson, Nancy and Paul Hittner, Gail and Ty Hongladarom / A Garden of Distinction, Gayle and Gary Hooker, Mr. and Mrs. Lance Ito, Kathy and Aldie Johnson, Lani and Larry Johnson / The Johnson Partnership, Janene and Michael Khanchalian, Donaleen Kohn and John Bressler, Lawrence Kreisman and Wayne Dodge, Mr. and Mrs. Wally Haas, Janie and William Jones, Paul Lanouette and James Stefanucci, Denise L. Lawrence, Ruth and Michael Mack, Aida Mancillas and Lynn Susholtz, Marilee Marshall and Bruce Wright, Fred Martin, Carol McCafferty, Maggie McDermott and Don Di Pietro, John McDonald, Cindy and Tim McGinn, Valerie and Kelly McKenzie, Pauline C. Metcalf, Sallie Middleton, Carol and Hal Moats, Valerie Bailey and Roger B. Mohling / R.B. Mohling Construction Company, David and Len Moore, Margaret and Michael Morales, Cynthia and George Null, Laura and John Olinski, Sharon Osmond, Carol Polansky and Michael Ratliff, Elizabeth Pomeroy, Tim Pylko, David Raposa and Ed Trosper / City Living Realty, Lisa and Scott Rines, Marjorie Romer, Phillip Rossi, Maxine and James Risley, Marnie Ross, Dolores and Dan Solaro, Claudia Sandler and Bill Levin, Jessie and Daniel Levin, Mara and Gregg Seibert, Julie and Raymond Snyder, Frances and Gary Spradlin, Alisa Taylor and Ron Hutchinson, Judith and John Tankard, Rebecca and Russ Teasdale, Kirk R. Thatcher, Marilyn Thomas and Jim Bixler, Kitty Turgeon and Robert Rust / Roycroft Shops, Inc., Mary F. Ward, Vreni and Jerry Watt, Elizabeth and Steve Westbrook, Martin Eli Weil, Zvia and Robert Weinstein / Craftsman Style, Connie and Mike Whalen, Michael Wheelden, Linda Brackins Willet and Robert E. Willet, Kelly and Phillip Woods, Larry Word and Don Bean, John Zanakis and Arthur van der Beek / House of Orange.

We would like to acknowledge those persons and organizations who directly or indirectly helped us with this project, and as many as possible have been included here. Their help took many forms, ranging from moral support to sharing useful ideas, resources, and location referrals. To each we offer our heartfelt thanks: Adams Design Associates, Inc. / Stephen Adams, Ainsley House / Campbell Historical Museum / Melissa Heyman, Alameda Victorian Preservation Society, Albany (Oregon) Visitors Association / Julie Jackson, City of Albany (Oregon) / Rosalind M. Keeney, Vonne Alvey, *American Bungalow* / John Brinkman and George Murray, Arroyo Style / Laurie King and David Heller, Artistic License of San Francisco, The Arts & Crafts Guild of Northern California, Arts & Crafts Period Textiles / Dianne Ayres and Timothy Hansen, The Arts & Crafts Press / *The Tabby* / Yoshiko Yamamoto and Bruce Smith, Bennye and Richard Bail, Arlene Baxter / Arts & Crafts Homes, John Benriter, Berkeley Architectural Heritage Association / Anthony Bruce, Becky Bernie, Vicky and Marshall Berol, Matthew Bialecki / Matthew Bialecki Associates, Terry Bible, Bill W. and Dr. Bob, Adrienne Bolsega, Nixon Borah, Edward R. Bosley and Gamble House staff, Helen Boutell, Elise Brewster and Paul Smith / Kallos, Bruce Bradbury / Bradbury & Bradbury Art Wallpapers and staff, Kathleen and Peter Bridgman, Susan Brillantes, Jane Browne, Bungalow Heaven Neighborhood Association, John Burrows / J.R. Burrows & Company, Mike Byrnes, Paula and Duncan Cameron, Jerry T. Campbell, Charles Cash, Scott Cazet, Robert Judson Clark, Coldwell Banker / 1st Borrego Springs Properties / Catherine B. Gay and Trudy Melvin, Regina Cole, Brian Coleman and Howard Cohen, The Craftsman Farms Foundation, Inc. / Lynn M. Leeb, Tommy A. McPherson II and Beth Ann McPherson, The Craftsman Home / Lee Jester and Marcia Leitner, Craftsman Style / Robert and Zvia Weinstein / Bridgid Faith, Rich Cromer and Jim Johnson, Dalton's American Decorative Arts / Debbie Goldwein Rudd and Dave Rudd, Rick Darke, Lori Delman, Scott Dolph, Riley Doty / Doty Tile, Kevin Dougherty, Ed Polk Douglas, Leon F. Drozd Jr., R. Geraldine and James P. Duchscherer, Kenneth J. Duchscherer, Sandy and Steven P. Duchscherer, Hank Dunlop / Victorian Preservation Center of Oakland / Cohen-Bray House, Sammie and Robert Dunn, Echo Park Historical Society, Bob Elston, Katarina Eriksson, Ewing Architects Inc. / Doug Ewing, Susan Federman, Foundation for the Study of the Arts & Crafts Movement at Roycroft / Kitty Turgeon and Robert Rust / Tisha Zawisky, Carol and Jack Fentiman, Lawrence Foy, Robin and Sydney Galer, Galvin + Cristilli Architects / James Galvin, Arrol Gellner, Ora Gosey, Vicki D. Granowitz and William R. Lees, Vykki Mende Gray and David Swarens, Dan Gregory / *Sunset* magazine, Jackie and Robert Gustafson, Austene Hall and Robert Archibald, Julie Hardgrove and Cliff Cline, Lucy Hardiman, Robert Herny, Denise, Keith, and Stephanie Hice, Richard Hilkert, Historic Preservation League of Oregon / Louise Gomez Burgess, Historic Seattle / Larry Kreisman, Historic Milwaukee / Sandy Ackerman, Monique Hoogenboom and Douglas Steiner, Glen Jarvis / Jarvis Architects, Bruce Johnson / Grove Park Inn Arts and Crafts Conference, Katherine Keister, Jacqui King, Mrs. Roland W. Klotz, Douglas Klotz, Robert Kneisel, Lina and Wayne Knowles, Gaylord Kubota, John Kurtz, Craig A. Kuhns, The Lanterman House / Melissa Patton, Jeanne and Mark Lazzarini, Lynn Lustberg, Kris Maas, Caro Macpherson, Janet Mark and Terry Geiser, Randell L. Makinson, Marston House / Lucinda Eddy, Peggy and Damian Martin, Jim N. Matsuo, Vonn Marie May, Claudia and James D. McCord, Lynne McDaniel, Roy McMakin, Carol Mead / Carol Mead Design, Don Miller, Mary Lou and Ron Miller, Fumi Momoto, Elizabeth A. Moore and Oger Owner, Jean and Roger Moss, Steve Moyer, Gretchen Muller, Brian Murrian, Museums of San Diego History / Victoria Newcomb, *North Park News* / Thomas Shess, Oakland Architectural Heritage Association, *Old House Interiors* / Gloucester Publishers / Patricia Poore, William O'Donnell and staff, *Old House Journal* / Hanley-Wood, Inc. / Patricia Poore / Gordon Bock and staff, Valorie Olsen, Pasadena Heritage / Onnolee Sullivan, Sheree Sampson and staff, Pasadena Junior Philharmonic Committee / Gretchen McNally / Pasadena Showcase House of Design 1998, Marsha Perloff, David Pennington, Catherine and Louis Phelps / Four Dimensions, Pinson and Ware / Ed Pinson and Debra Ware, Bonnie Poppe, Jared Polsky & Associates / David Ludwig, Jane Powell / House Dressing, Preservation Society of Asheville / Harry Weiss, Betsy Priddy and Jimmy Onstott, Morris Potter, Anne Purcell, Jeanne Purcell, Kathy Purcell, Rejuvenation Lamp and Fixture Company / Jim Kelly and staff, Julie Reiz and Ken Miedema, Steve Rham, Debra Richards, Michael Robert, Chuck Roche and Joseph Ryan, Matthew Romanelli, Charles Rupert Designs / Margaret Graham-Bell and Stuart Stark, Sacramento Bungalow Heritage Association / Susan and Steve Ballew, Enid Thompson Sales, Al E. Saroyan II, Save Our Heritage Organization / San Diego, Mr. and Mrs. Chris Schwemmer, Joan Seear, Jane Shabaker, Cathy Shadd and Dov Rosenfeld, Robin Schifflet, Sigma Phi Society / William R. Thorsen house / David Salazar, RAI/EGI Exhibitions, Inc., Sherrie Somers, Inga Sonderberg, Style: 1900 / David Rago and staff, James E. Sullivan, Lawrence Sullivan, Sunnyside / Historic Hudson Valley / Dina R. Friedman and Timothy Steinhoff, Many Ann Witte, Ray Stubblebine, Pat Suzuki, Juliet and Charles Sykes, Laurie Taylor / Ivy Hill Interiors, Marty and Ron Thomas, Susan and Tony Thompson, Tile Restoration Center / Marie Glasse Tapp and Delia Tapp, Toyon Design / Richard W. Fisher, ASLA, Traditional Building / Clem Labine and Judith Lief, Victorian Preservation Association of San Jose, The Victorian Society in America, Jane and William L. Veen, Gladys Nereyda Arebalo Vides and Elder Vides / Painting Concepts, Marti J. Wachtel, Catherine P. Wells, West Adams Historical Association, Richard Guy Wilson, Dr. Robert Winter, Phil Wood, Jim and Julie Woodward, Julie and Lance Wright, Debey Zito and Terry Schmitt.

Immeasurable thanks to our patient and caring editor, Cyril Nelson, whose wealth of book experience, personal interest in Arts and Crafts design, and commitment to this project has contributed greatly to the final result. Special thanks are extended to our literary agent, Julie Castiglia / The Castiglia Agency, for expert advice, counsel, and encouragement. Finally, our deepest gratitude is humbly offered to Sandy Schweitzer, John Freed, and Don Merrill, whose generosity of spirit is reflected in their invaluable feedback, continuous moral support, and exceptional patience and understanding.

Preface

A Look Back and Forward

This book is the third volume in a series that celebrates the enduring appeal of the bungalow. More popular today than at any time since the early twentieth century, its revival shows no signs of slowing down for the new century. In part, this renewed popularity was jumpstarted by a concurrent return of interest in the Arts and Crafts Movement, one of the bungalow's most significant design influences. But perhaps the rediscovery has more to do with modern life; for while bungalows make ideal period settings for collections of Arts and Crafts objects and furnishings, they are also quite accommodating to more contemporary tastes.

The first book in the series, *The Bungalow: America's Arts & Crafts Home*, covered the bungalow's history, its various architectural styles, and showed interior views of many examples. In response to a strong reader demand for more interior coverage, *Inside the Bungalow: America's Arts & Crafts Interior* followed, and explored that subject room by room, in greater detail. Once again, encouraged by persuasive reader feedback, the garden now takes the spotlight as an integral part of bungalow living.

Some readers may recognize familiar locations included in this book, as a few of them have appeared in one (or both) of the first two books; these have been noted accordingly. Those garden elements that are common to one location, but presented in separate chapters, have also been cross-referenced to each other.

Rather than emphasizing the selection and use of plants, the focus of this book is on the fixed architectural or "hardscape" elements that are used to form, shape, and define outdoor living spaces. The Introduction's historic overview contrasts Victorian garden precedent with the emergence of a new sensibility: how the garden could be an expression of the Arts and Crafts Movement. Highlighted are the primary sources of this phenomenon, and how their influence appeared in America's bungalow gardens.

It is the Movement's design sensibility, particularly linked with Craftsman-style bungalows, which pervades most of the examples throughout this book. To illustrate a greater diversity, some examples are also included that reflect the Colonial Revival, English Tudor or Cottage, and Mission or Spanish Colonial Revival styles.

Although evidence of the public's growing penchant for historic-revival styles, particularly throughout the Twenties, it should be noted that many of these later bungalows still featured some Craftsman influence in their gardens. This is testimony to how versatile and compatible this "nature-friendly" design influence can be in almost any garden.

As with missing exterior or interior architectural elements of bungalows, illuminating solutions for gardens are to be found in illustrations and drawings taken from books, magazines and related product catalogs of the period. As many as possible have been included.

Particularly atmospheric and evocative of the bungalow glory days are views reproduced from early colored postcards of the period. These fascinating images, commonly exchanged by friends and relatives as mementos of early twentieth-century road trips, portray these homes in a romantic glow. It is notable that such postcards were, for a time, the way that many Americans glimpsed their first bungalow. Whether by the houses or their garden settings, many recipients were apparently captivated, and such postcards contributed to making "bungalowmania" a nationwide obsession for almost three decades.

This book's format was conceived as a walk through

the garden; along the way, some of the most frequently confounding garden-design problems are confronted. Individual chapters follow, with an array of garden ideas, and potential solutions:

"Garden Portraits" features striking ensembles of various elements working together. In a variety of styles, many of these gardens are viewed in context with their houses.

"Approaching the Garden" is full of ideas of many shapes and sizes for garden gates.

"Enclosing the Garden" shows a variety of forms and materials for fences and walls.

"Traversing the Garden" explores a range of solutions for paths, walkways, and steps.

"Cooling the Garden" highlights the different types and uses of water elements.

"Furnishing the Garden" ponders a wide spectrum of outdoor furniture possibilities.

"In the Greene and Greene Garden" shows overall views and details taken in the gardens of several different California houses designed by Charles and Henry Greene. While their homes have come to exemplify American Arts and Crafts design at its most exalted, the gardens surrounding them offer surprisingly practical ideas, some of which have potential for application in the most modest of bungalow gardens.

"Details in the Garden" enumerates and addresses the needs of other garden categories with multiple options. Many period examples are among those illustrating a broad variety of architectural elements, outdoor lighting fixtures, and related garden accessories.

"Planting the Garden" has an extensive plant list, contemporary to the Arts and Crafts period, arranged for various applications. This will be of particular interest to those curious to know about popular planting selections of early twentieth-century gardens.

For the greatest diversity, examples for this book were photographed in as many different locales as possible. Unlike the selection of plants, which must be geared to specific climatic zones, the design of a garden's fixed architectural features can transcend location.

Although first conceived to inform and inspire prospective or current bungalow homeowners, the audience for these books has extended further. Many readers don't live in bungalows, but do collect Arts and Crafts furnishings; it seems that a greater familiarity with homes of a similar style or period helps them to imagine more distinctly the original settings of their treasures. Others, who are not necessarily collectors, seek to adapt some of the architectural or design ideas found in vintage bungalows to a more modern or newly constructed home. Some people enjoy these books because they trigger fond memories of their childhood or of old friends.

Among the newest fans of these homes are younger people. For many, whose childhoods were spent in blandly anonymous suburban settings, the charm and character of such older, quirkier housing can be appealing. In fact, some of today's most ardent bungalow fans are people who didn't know a thing about them, until one fateful day they stumbled into one as an unwitting renter, and soon became smitten.

Others are interested in them for even more practical reasons. A good working background in historic housing styles makes sense for architecture, design, or construction-industry professionals, for bungalows comprise a fast-growing segment of the restoration and renovation marketplace.

Perhaps the bungalow fires so many of our imaginations because it reads like an archetypically American movie: from humble beginnings, tinged with artistic idealism, came unprecedented popularity; then, through aggressive development, big business interests pushed its limits; eventually, in the wake of changing popular taste, its star faded. Perhaps it is because a sense of romance, missing from the present, may be gleaned from backward glances. This is surely part of an intangible lure that keeps so many old-house fans and owners so intrigued and dedicated.

The compulsion to improve one's own garden extends far beyond the style or age of a house. The human response to a garden environment tends to be far more consistent than to housing styles. For despite what a home may look like, the view out a window or through a doorway into the garden can be perceived as more of a blank slate: one that invites participation, interpretation, and perhaps a level of experimentation that might never be applied to the house. For whether or not it belongs to a bungalow, a garden has a life of its own, and can trigger universal responses of wonder and delight.

PAUL DUCHSCHERER

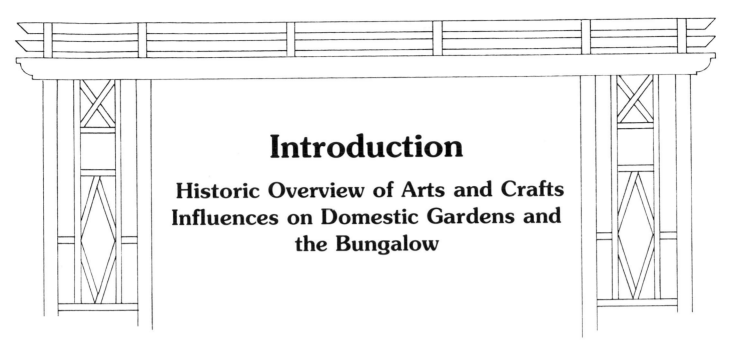

Introduction

Historic Overview of Arts and Crafts Influences on Domestic Gardens and the Bungalow

Before Arts and Crafts: Victorian Gardens

Historically, in both England and America, the arts have been an influential force in determining what constitutes good taste or is perceived as fashionable. Throughout the nineteenth century, a heavy veil of romance colored the public's prevailing tastes in art as well as music and literature; other notions of romance were popularly expressed through the historic revivalism of Victorian architecture.

A similar approach was also used in shaping other design trends of the day, such as illogically ornate furniture and the profusion of decorative *objets d'art* that crowded the typical Victorian parlor. For those who strove to be admired or fashion-conscious, quantity could easily eclipse quality in the "Age of the Collector."

The taste for plants mirrored the decorative objects. Calculated to impress, it was especially desirable to maintain a collection of rare, unusual, or exotic plants, preferably showcased in a conspicuously visible greenhouse. Many Victorians considered the garden an outdoor counterpart to their parlor.

In evidence in the vast majority of their gardens was a compulsion to harness and control nature. For fear of making their garden appear neglected or forlorn, most people avoided any garden effect that appeared too loosely naturalistic or wild. Instead of being a place for the free expression of natural beauty, Victorian social conventions dictated that the garden should be a decorative frame or backdrop for the house.

Many homeowners were inspired by the impressive flower beds seen in public parks. For those who could afford their upkeep there was a decidedly strong preference for beds with formalized, geometric outlines arranged on carefully trimmed, sprawling lawns. Inspired by the formalized Renaissance or Baroque gardens, beds could also affect more whimsical, curvilinear shapes. In the later 1860s, the term *carpet bedding* was used to describe those beds that were densely planted with varieties of dwarf or creeping foliage plants, trained into a uniform carpet-like surface, and perhaps outlined or accented with the contrasting leaves of succulents to form decorative patterns. Whatever the overall arrangement, order and symmetry were favored. For the showiest impact, beds were usually filled with neatly installed rows of closely spaced plants that were densely grouped according to color. For added drama, plantings were sometimes selected and placed to exploit strongly contrasting colors and textures.

The most fashionable garden accessories were cast iron or concrete lawn decorations frequently painted white for emphasis. Popular forms included widely reproduced figures of demure goddesses and other classically inspired statuary. Pairs of classical urns used to punctuate an entry walk or terminate a view were frequently bursting with bright red geraniums. Subtlety was unpopular in most Victorian gardens: usually the more vivid the colors, or the more intoxicating the fragrances, the better.

Appearing to be irregular constructions of tree branches, so-called "rustic" furniture for the garden had appeared in English and American gardens by the mid-nineteenth century. When they first appeared, such designs were most likely to be made of cast iron. Some variations on the rustic theme incorporated naturalistic motifs other than tree branches, although cast-iron benches designed with fern leaves, trailing ivy, or dangling grapevines were even less likely to produce convincing structural effects.

The use of one material to look like another is a typical Victorian conceit that was representative of many mass-produced, machine-made products so emblematic of the Industrial Revolution. Since symmetry dominated most Victorian design, the appearance of "rustic" garden accessories is sometimes mistakenly perceived as due to an Arts and Crafts influence. Squarely against the grain of the Arts and Crafts sensibility, such an approach to design would have been subject to harsh criticism by its proponents for being dishonest in its representation of nature and flagrantly manipulative of public taste.

Roots of the Arts and Crafts Garden: England and William Morris

In searching out the roots of the Arts and Crafts garden, it is necessary to consider first the sources of the Arts and Crafts Movement. Its earliest manifestation was in England, and, if its influence on gardens is somewhat less celebrated than its philosophy or the austere richness of its decorative arts and architecture, it is still undeniable.

Most notably a force that promoted design reform, the Movement began in the mid-nineteenth century against a backdrop of the burgeoning Industrial Revolution. Its reforming premises evolved out of a sense of urgency to save age-old traditions of English crafts and handwork, many of which were rapidly degenerating or threatening to disappear under the advancing cloud of mechanization.

A major part of the Movement's less artistic side was the concern that industrial workers were losing an essential part of their humanity, if not their souls, in exchange for the assurance of low but steady wages from high-profit industrial concerns.

While the Movement had many devoted disciples over its most active period of about sixty years, it never achieved their hoped-for level of influence or mainstream momentum in industry. Considering the nearly full-blown state of its conceptual thinking close to mid-century, it is notable that the Movement's name as we know it was not officially coined until 1888, when the Arts and Crafts Exhibition Society was formed in London.

William Morris (1834–1896), the person most associated with the roots of the Arts and Crafts Movement, is sometimes referred to as its "father," and often credited with its founding; indeed, Morris was to become one of the greatest and most influential cultural figures in English history. He accomplished much in sixty-two years as a visionary artist, designer, craftsman, poet, writer, teacher, preservationist, business entrepreneur, and political activist.

Born into a prosperous family, he could readily afford to cultivate his budding intellectual and artistic inclinations without financial obstacles or even much family resistance. Later in life, his inclinations toward social reform found him increasingly devoted to assisting the less fortunate to improve their lives, and actively promoting Socialism as a viable solution to many of the industrialized world's chronic problems.

During his college years at Oxford, Morris came to believe that the values that had brought an intense focus and commitment to the work of artisans and craftsmen of the Middle Ages could be a model to live by in the modern world. He felt that such an ideal fusion of work and art in the daily lives of working people would lead to higher consciousness, deeper spirituality, and a better, more satisfying life. Variations on this way of thinking and approach to work is central to any definition of the Arts and Crafts philosophy.

Morris's idealized vision of the Middle Ages was fueled in part by his early association with a group of renegade painters, who called themselves the Pre-Raphaelite Brotherhood. Prominent among its members were Dante Gabriel Rossetti (1828–1882), William Holman Hunt (1827–1910), John Everett Millais (1829–1896), Arthur Hughes (1832–1915), and Edward Burne-Jones (1833–1998). Collectively, they sought to revive the lost richness and spiritual depth of medieval painting, which was contrary to the then-Classical orientation of mainstream art. Reflecting their philosophy, their paintings were intense, finely crafted, richly detailed, and were prone to themes of morality. Conveyed through allegorical meanings and Arthurian legends, the Pre-Raphaelite painters produced numerous images of people in Medieval-style clothing, set against meticulously rendered natural backgrounds, particularly woodland scenes. For a time, their work and vision inspired Morris to try his own hand at painting.

He soon realized that his greater talent lay in designing beautiful and complex repeating patterns based on stylized plant forms, which he drew from life. He was moved by the mysterious beauties of nature, particularly the structure and color of favorite flowers. Morris was also influenced by illuminated manuscripts of the Middle Ages and by the delicate designs of flowers and vines used in embroidery of that period. Eventually produced by hand as block-printed wallpapers and fabrics, the masterful patterns he created stood out from the excess-ridden taste of

1. Front porch of a bungalow in San Diego, California (1910). Above the shady porch of this 1910 Craftsman-style home, the upswept turn of the gable's peak suggests an Oriental influence. Buffered from the street by a flowery profusion in the front yard, the porch is surrounded by a movable collection of potted plants, succulents, and cacti, which blend into the fixed plantings. Trained up the column at the right, the variegated cream and green leaves of a *Bougainvillea glabra* set off its papery, magenta bracts. These plantings thrive in the region's Mediterranean climate. (For other views of this house see figs. 67-69; also *The Bungalow*, fig. 119.)

the Victorian era. Although the patterns were complex, their undulating movement and subtlety of color emanate a calm, unpretentious beauty.

In addition to designing patterns, Morris became a lecturer on and teacher of various crafts; he was particularly skilled at weaving, embroidery, and working with dyes. Late in his life he founded the Kelmscott Press, which published limited editions of finely crafted, handprinted books of strikingly beautiful graphic design. Best known is *The Works of Geoffrey Chaucer* (1896), a collaboration with artist and lifelong close friend Edward Burne-Jones.

Morris had a knack for coordinating other people's energies, and then inspiring them into productive directions. As a direct result of his decision to build a country house and of the ensuing collaborations with others who were needed to design, build, and furnish it, a pivotal moment in his life occurred.

Motivated by their disdain for the low level of craftsmanship and design that was to be found in commercial home furnishings, they believed they could design and produce finer material for the public. In 1861, several of the artistically motivated colleagues who had helped Morris create his house were incorporated in a business venture that would function as a decorating firm and also produce interior furnishings. First called Morris, Marshall, Faulkner and Company, "The Firm" (as it was called by them) became Morris and Company by 1875.

Including a variety of beautiful, useful, well-designed, and handcrafted furniture, metalwork, ceramics, stained glass, textiles, and wallpapers, much of the work was custom-designed and created for specific installations. Inspired by the strength and integrity of the medieval design they all admired, stained glass for churches was a mainstay for the firm. Their products for the home were destined to become fashionable with an affluent clientele.

An original goal of the Morris firm had been to reach the homes of the general public by offering high-quality workmanship at affordable prices. This proved to be more idealistic than realistic and was especially frustrating to Morris. Despite a slim profit margin, the prices that had to be charged for their handcrafted goods made them unaffordable for most of the households they had hoped to improve.

Early Arts and Crafts: The Red House Garden

Although they only occupied it for about six years, the new country house created for William Morris and his young bride, Jane Burden, would always be fondly associated with the firm's beginnings. Not far from London, it was situated at Bexleyheath in Kent and named the Red House for the soft red color of its brick walls and handmade clay-

tile roof. Its architect was Morris's close friend and associate Philip Webb (1831–1915), but there must also have been considerable design input from Morris, who had studied architecture. Most of the planning for the house was completed by 1859.

Foreshadowing the work of future English Arts and Crafts architects, Webb's projects were destined to become influential and admired for creatively adapting vernacular building styles and materials to new architectural designs. Despite the comfortable familiarity of its traditional materials and Gothic forms used for windows and detailing, the Red House was a landmark project. Sometimes called one of the first "modern" houses, it was conceived and built as a unified expression of its owner's taste and needs, and it helped to define Arts and Crafts design.

From the project's onset, both Webb and Morris were committed to designing a house that was appropriate to, as well as interactive with, its setting. An existing orchard, characteristic of Kent's regional landscape, was chosen as the site for the Red House. Within the confines of its grounds one of the first Arts and Crafts gardens was created.

Considering the house and garden as a unified whole reflected a distinct departure from the typical mid-Victorian approach, which emphasized separation between indoor and outdoor activities. Instead, the Red House and garden bridged them, extended by a series of outdoor living spaces. Apparently no overall landscaping plans were drawn for the Red House, but some garden-related notes remain on parts of its original plan and elevation drawings. Locations are referenced for specific plants, including fragrant white jasmine, honeysuckle, climbing rose, and passion-flower to grow on trellises placed against the building.

For variety of outlook, sun exposure, and use, covered porches were placed at both the north and south sides of the house to create intimate, sheltered outdoor sitting areas. Morris playfully called the south-facing one The Pilgrim's Rest, a reference to the route taken through the area by the pilgrims described in Chaucer's *Canterbury Tales*. While none of the primary living spaces of the house opened directly onto the garden (as they often do in bungalows), the views either from the house or toward it were carefully considered. This is reflected in the calculated placement of the L-shape design of the house, which zoned the garden's spaces into distinctly different areas.

Brightened by its orientation to the east and south through large windows overlooking the garden, the main interior stairway was expressed on the exterior as a fanciful Gothic tower. Its position at the inside turn of the L was flanked by the two asymmetrical wings, which gave the house a sense of having been constructed or added to over

2. Arbor-covered front gate of the Cook house in San Diego, California (1911). Set close to the sidewalk across a shallow front yard, this shingled bungalow needed additional shielding from the street. To preserve its welcoming feeling, the present owner designed this lattice fence with a large entry gate that implies privacy without entirely blocking the view of the front door. The house was originally built in the Mission Hills neighborhood for Allen B. Cook and designed by the architectural partnership (1910–1912) of Emmor Brooke Weaver and John Terrell Vawter. Climbing roses named *Cecile Brunner*, a favorite of the period, have been trained to form a fragrantly dense covering for the spreading arbor.

3. Rustic arbor and gardener's cottage (c.1895) at Sunnyside (1835–1850), Tarrytown, New York. Made with unpeeled logs and branches, this well-crafted rustic arbor forms a picturesque support for climbing roses that will shade a garden path beneath. Situated at Sunnyside, the historic home of famed American writer Washington Irving, this cottage and its garden are located uphill from the main house that overlooks the Hudson River. Maintained as a kitchen garden that might have existed during Irving's time, this view shows how ornamental plants are integrated into the same area used for vegetables. Sunnyside and its grounds are open to the public. (For other views see figs. 98, 282, 283.)

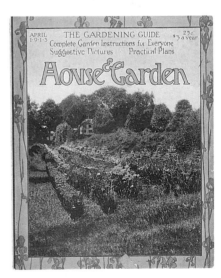

4. Cover of *House & Garden* magazine, April 1913. This national periodical was one of several that helped to mold the gardening and design trends of bungalow homeowners. This issue's articles covered such topics as vegetable and flower gardening, trees and shrubbery, the use of ornamental vines on houses, and buying garden equipment, along with coverage of interior lighting ideas, and a model house and its garden. The editor, Henry H. Saylor, was also well known for his 1911 book called *Bungalows*.

5. The Roycroft Blacksmith Shop, now the Roycroft Shops, East Aurora, New York (1902). When he created this building for the Roycroft community, Elbert Hubbard paid homage to the English Arts and Crafts Movement by adapting some of its architectural forms. Nearly engulfed in the rampant tendrils of Boston ivy *(Parthenocissus tricuspidata)*, the walls are built of local stone, and its original roof has clay tiles that were handmade at the famous ceramics division of Alfred University in Alfred, New York. Peeking out of the gable end, the timbers of an angled truss are set into stucco in a half-timbered style typical of the medieval-inspired Tudor Revival. Created in the spirit of an English cottage garden, the mixed-perennial bed in the foreground includes the orange blooms of Siberian wallflower *(Erysimum aspe-rum)* in the foreground and tall, pale purple Siberian iris *(Iris siberica)* at the left. This building houses the Roycroft Shops, Inc., which exhibit the new work of Roycroft Renaissance Artisans. (For other views see figs. 144, 251, 275, 278, 279, 281.)

a period of time. A picturesque round brick well, whose conical clay-tile roof and pointed finial restated the materials of the house, was placed at the center of a courtyard-like space. Its other two sides were defined by "walls" of open wooden trelliswork and a profusion of climbing roses.

Morris preferred separation from the outside world, so a high brick wall was built along the property line parallel to the public road. A gentler sense of enclosure was implied elsewhere by low fences and hedges entwined with roses and sweetbriar. Medieval in feeling and plan, square beds formed a quadrant interconnected by pathways punctuated with rose-covered arbors. On the west side of the house an open lawn area allowed for more distant views into the neighboring rural landscape. It also created a large play area used for lawn bowling and social gatherings.

Some of the existing orchard's rows of fruit trees were retained to lend their orderly structure to a series of linear, gravel-covered walkways, which stretched between beds of fragrant rosemary and lavender. An inventory noted that apples, cherries, plums, and hawthorns were among the eighty trees in the orchard. The careful siting of the house required only a few of these to be removed. Their mature character was prized by Morris and Webb, for it made the garden appear well-established and feel years older.

Few plantings can offer so much diversity of seasonal plenty as fruit trees: in spring, their bursting buds and clouds of blossoms give way to summer's shade; by autumn, fruit-laden boughs will soon be transformed into beautifully bleak and gnarled winter silhouettes. This scenario reinforces an enduring and useful Arts and Crafts garden-design sensibility: whether spectacular and showy, or subtle and moody, nature's beauty should be seen and savored in all seasons.

Influence of Morris

Many of those drawn to the work of Morris and Company were proponents of the Aesthetic Movement. A design-reform movement mostly of the 1870s and 1880s, its intentions lacked the clarity of focus and moralistic values of the Arts and Crafts philosophy. Its influence was mostly directed toward interior design and the decorative arts. Restrained adaptations of furniture and objects derived from sources including Gothic and Medieval designs were models of Aesthetic taste; also important influences were designs of the Middle and Far East, especially Japan.

Central to the focus of the Aesthetic Movement was the importance of creating unified interior-design schemes by careful selection of objects and furnishings chosen for their artistic integrity. All things ordinary and mediocre should be banished from one's domestic environment and replaced with objects of art and beauty. This thinking was championed by Charles Locke Eastlake, who wrote about it in his landmark design-advice book of 1868, *Hints on Household Taste*. It was less officially, but more flamboyantly, presented by Oscar Wilde, who freely dispensed design advice along with witticisms on the international lecture circuit. Not surprisingly, its adherents' intentions were widely misunderstood by many average middle-class people, who often perceived the aesthetes' attitudes to be snobbish or condescending.

If some negative concern about the Aesthetic Movement by the middle class was carried over to Morris and Company, it isn't surprising; for many perceived Morris and his associates to be artistic bohemians. Their idiosyncrasies were well-publicized and sometimes satirized in popular magazines such as *Punch*, and the so-called medieval dress of "Aesthetic" women, such as Jane Morris, helped to define Aesthetic fashion. While the Aesthetic Movement shared some Arts and Crafts ideas concerning the importance of design reform, it was missing the strong craft-versus-machine posture, and the accompanying component of social reform.

Nevertheless, the Aesthetic Movement paved the way for greater public interest in more progressive, non-historic styles, beginning with Art Nouveau and the later Arts and Crafts efforts. It was profoundly influential to the entire Western world, for it helped to popularize Japan, recently reopened to trade, as a fertile source for both art goods and design ideas. Popularly perceived as a refreshing breath of air from the earlier Victorian preoccupation with historicism, the spell of Japan would become a key influence on American Arts and Crafts architecture, interiors, and gardens, particularly apparent in the architectural and design work of Charles and Henry Greene and Frank Lloyd Wright.

A number of communally minded craft guilds were inspired by the example of Morris. Among the best known was the Guild of Handicraft, founded in 1888 by C.R. Ashbee in London. When Ashbee, in search of a more peaceful working environment, moved the Guild's operations from London to rural Chipping Campden, it set the tone for other small, self-contained crafts communities to relocate to the countryside. Disillusioned by life in the cities, some imagined liberation in an idyllic setting, where a new life could commence and sales of their crafts would provide the necessary sustenance. The sense of self-sufficient independence associated with growing one's own food had great appeal to those with utopian urges, but newly surrounded by an agriculture-based economy, most weren't prepared for the reality of a hand-to-mouth existence. Finding it necessary to become gardeners and farmers simply in order to eat, many made plans to escape back to the city. The ones who stayed on usually had the means to hire help for the less pleasant tasks, thus ensuring their garden's production.

The Cottage Garden: An Arts and Crafts Model

Used in abundance in the Red House garden, many old-fashioned flowering plants could also be found in England's cottage gardens. Their timeless charms in some ways reflect the simple and direct appeal of folk art. The straightforward design of cottage gardens was adapted by the Arts and Crafts world, particularly the garden experts William Robinson and Gertrude Jekyll. The welcoming informality of cottage gardens was widely admired and imitated in both England and America, and their qualities would prove to be of far-reaching influence on many Arts and Crafts gardens.

Traditionally, old-fashioned plants found in cottage gardens were often exchanged between friends and neighbors, rather than purchased, so many varieties were thus preserved over the years. Cottage favorites of William Morris were hollyhocks, sunflowers, various lilies, and daisies, all of which were planted in abundance at the Red House. The sunflower and lily became widely recognized symbols of the Aesthetic Movement, and Japanesque stylizations of their motifs appeared in many of that Movement's decorative arts.

Often enclosed by a low wall or hedge, cottage gardens were located at the front of the house. The entrance, possibly through a garden gate, might be defined by the dark green of a yew tree trained and clipped into an archway, but it could also be created by manipulating the rangy branches of a flowering quince. This "living archway" could also be created by using a simple construction of posts, or possibly a trellis, to support flowering vines.

Within, planted areas could be found as beds or borders, either lining the paths or set against the walls of the house. Lawns were not part of the cottage-garden; the entire front yard might be devoted to flowers. Fruit trees and flowering shrubs were frequently used, and sometimes the fruit trees, like pear or plum, were *espaliered*, meaning that they were trained to grow against the sunniest walls of the house. This was a decorative and useful way to save space.

Layouts for larger cottage gardens usually consisted of a series of planting beds that were outlined by paths laid in straight lines. Most paths were unpaved and finished with pounded earth, but some were covered with gravel, brick, or stone.

Serving as anchor plantings in most cottage gardens, clumps or rows of sturdy perennials or biennials were strategically placed. These were interspersed with a variety of hardy, dependable flowering annuals, which were likely to reseed themselves. Mixed planting beds could offer an ongoing show throughout the blooming season.

While many cottage gardens took advantage of extra space or sun exposure to grow a variety of edibles, they were generally conceived on a smaller scale than the plots set aside for vegetables, which were commonly known as kitchen gardens. Although most kitchen gardens were planned strictly for function, they had their own kind of beauty, and their seasonal changes were more dramatic. Usually, their need for greater scale and the activities involved in their ongoing maintenance (such as plowing) determined that the kitchen garden be away from the house.

Some of the renewed attention paid to the cottage garden in the late nineteenth century was due to successful, largely urban-based middle-class people discovering the pleasures of a second home. Downturns in Britain's agricultural economy had made country properties financially attractive. This turn to the country was especially appealing to artistic or literary types, for many simple farm cottages were available on a full-time basis and suited their needs and modest budgets. There appeared to be an element of romance in rural cottages and gardens that wouldn't have occurred to most of the previous occupants, and public interest in them was aroused.

At about this same time America's middle class also became aware of the appeal of a cottage or vacation home. Well-recognized and potent symbols of domestic coziness by the Twenties, the English cottage and its romanticized garden became very popular models for America's later bungalows.

William Robinson: A Return to Nature

Born in Ireland, William Robinson (1838–1935), a lifelong gardener and self-taught botanist, is best known as a writer, who passionately promoted the use of native English plants in gardens and landscaping. His contributions to the Arts and Crafts Movement developed through his influence on its gardens. Appalled by the common custom of changing bedding plants twice in a growing season, Robinson felt it would be better to incorporate planting schemes that were lower in maintenance. He became highly influential, and fundamentally changed much of the public's perception of garden development.

Early in his career, he gained much practical experience working in large public gardens, first in Dublin at the National Botanic Garden, then in London at the Royal Botanic Society's garden in Regent's Park. It was there, while in charge of tending a garden area of native plants, that he became enamored with them. It became a lifelong

6. View of the main house at Craftsman Farms, Parsippany-Troy Hills, New Jersey (1911). Here one of the massive stone chimneys and some diamond-paned dormer windows of Gustav Stickley's beloved home are glimpsed as part of a verdant tapestry. The small pond's waters are strewn with water lilies, and boulders at its edge create a perch for surveying the serene scene. Its atmosphere is still powerfully evocative of the romantic vision Gustav Stickley had for Craftsman Farms, where a simply built environment for learning and enjoyment could merge with the beauty and peace of nature.

7. Corner of the main house at Craftsman Farms, Parsippany-Troy Hills, New Jersey (1911). This pleasantly shaded outdoor living area adjoins a long glassed-in porch, which stretches across the downhill side of the house, capturing more light and open views for the interior. A two-piece Dutch door leads to the terrace from the porch. Visible in the foreground is a round granite millstone that was set into the flagstone paving as a decorative accent. Planting beds that surround the house are edged with large stones.

8. Main house at Craftsman Farms, Parsippany-Troy Hills, New Jersey (1911). This house, sited on a rise over-looking the densely wooded landscape seen at left, is now open to the public as the Stickley Museum. Seemingly rooted to the ground by its massive chimneys, the house was constructed with chestnut logs and granite. The first-floor interior has rough-hewn walls of exposed logs and oversize copper-hooded fireplaces. In the single-story wing at right, the unusually large kitchen recalls Stickley's original plan for this building to be a club house for his farm-and-craft school.

9. Detail of stone walls and steps at Craftsman Farms, Parsippany-Troy Hills, New Jersey (1911). Rising gently toward the main house, these stone steps and stone retaining walls define two levels of open lawn. Made of the same stone as the foundation and chimneys of the house, the steps and walls expand the connection of the building to the landscape and make a graceful transition to the surrounding natural woodland. Early photographs show that the steps were once covered with a rustic wooden arbor for flowering vines, and the stone walls were lined with planting beds. (For other views see figs. 6-8, 257.)

10. Cover of *Garden Magazine & Home Builder*, August 1925. Dappled sunlight on a shingled wall and a window box planted with trailing nasturtiums make an alluring image for the cover of this popular gardening and home-design magazine. By 1925, the popularity of the Colonial Revival had eclipsed that of the Craftsman style, as can be seen in the traditional styling of the window and the paler paint colors. In addition to garden-related topics, the magazine contains such bungalow-related articles as "Fabrics for the Homelike House," "The Evolution of the American Porch," and "The Perfect Little Maidless House."

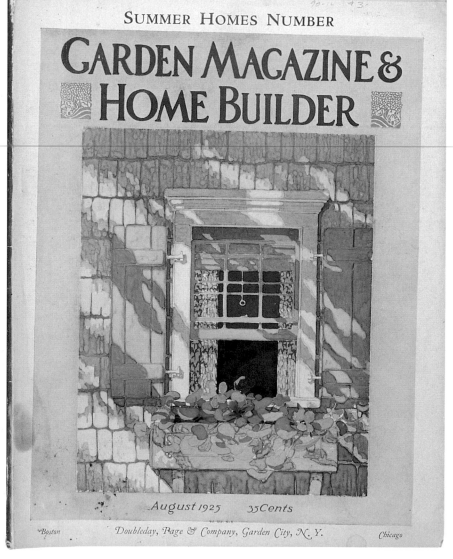

SUMMER HOMES NUMBER

GARDEN MAGAZINE & HOME BUILDER

August 1925   35 Cents

Boston   Doubleday, Page & Company, Garden City, N. Y.   Chicago

interest, and inspired him to inform others of their beauty and relevance to gardens of that period. He expressed his ideas through writing, and by the late 1860's Robinson was the horticultural correspondent to *The Times*.

Although not the first writer to promote the use of native plants, he was probably the most effective at making his point. In his best known book, *The Wild Garden*, published in 1870, he startled both gardening amateurs and professionals with his strong opinion about the underrated and underutilized charms of indigenous bulbs, shrubs, and perennials. Another basic premise of the book was that gardens should reflect the beauties of the season, as nature intended them, and gardens so planned could also greatly reduce their maintenance requirements. His ideas were heard loudly in Britain and America, for many found his naturalistic approach to landscape design and reverence for native plants to be both logical and appropriate. *The Wild Garden* was extremely successful, and it has remained a reference mainstay of garden libraries.

In 1871, Robinson founded a popular weekly periodical called *The Garden* through which, for many years, he was able to share his ideas with an avid following. *The English Flower Garden*, an important compilation of articles assembled from the ensuing years of *The Garden*, was published in 1883. It became another long-selling landmark book that helped to fuel Robinson's other endeavors.

Although he came from a modest background, the great popularity of his writings enabled him to realize significant financial success. As a result, in 1885 he was able to acquire Gravetye Manor, an Elizabethan stone mansion in West Hoathley, East Sussex, that was the centerpiece of a large country estate. Eventually, Robinson was able to acquire additional surrounding land, finally accumulating almost a thousand acres. Over the next fifty years, the grounds and gardens of Gravetye Manor became the ultimate proving ground for his gardening concepts. In 1911, Robinson published a book that traced his progress in transforming the grounds of Gravetye Manor from Victorian confusion into a practical working model of "wild gardening."

Before the turn of the century, most serious garden design in America was geared toward either public parks or estates of the wealthy, who could afford the high costs of maintenance by a gardening staff. The designs for such serious gardening in America were generally copied from grand British traditions or other European sources such as France and Italy. Well into the twentieth century, the upper levels of society on both sides of the Atlantic continued to favor the kind of control over nature and pretentious approach to garden design that Robinson despised.

Over his long life, Robinson associated with many of the most important advocates of design reform in England. Prominent among these was the art critic, philosopher, and writer John Ruskin (1819–1900), a pivotal figure who championed the causes of the Pre-Raphaelites, William Morris, and many others in the Arts and Crafts Movement. Robinson was a major influence on Gertrude Jekyll, who began her writing career with articles for *The Garden*, leading her to become one of the most prolific and popular garden writers and garden designers in England. They shared many of the same ideas, as well as mutual admiration and respect. In 1900, almost three decades after founding it, Robinson entrusted her with the editorial responsibilities of *The Garden*.

While the influence of Robinson took decades to have a mainstream effect, it became important early in the American Arts and Crafts Movement. Many of its members gardened for themselves (but on a smaller scale), were avid readers of Robinson, and concurred with his ideas. Although some of the planting issues differed, his concepts translated well to our shores. Working with nature, rather than against it, seemed to be less radical and to make more common sense in America, as did the idea of creating a garden within the framework of a natural landscape. These became some of the basic tenets of the American Arts and Crafts garden, as it began to emerge in the early twentieth century.

Gertrude Jekyll: The Arts and Crafts Gardener

Few women of her era had a career as accomplished as that of Gertrude Jekyll (pronounced "*Gee*-kull," 1843–1932), who grew up in a time when any form of professional self-expression for "respectable" women was discouraged, and even sometimes actively suppressed. Her best-known association with the Arts and Crafts Movement was as a garden designer, and her primary legacy is based on the far-reaching success of her many books and articles about gardening.

She was fortunate to be born into a forward-thinking, upper-middle-class London family that nurtured her independence and creative interests from an early age. Her own roots in gardening probably stem from before the age of five, when she and her family moved to a large country estate near the village of Bramley in Surrey. There she seems to have enjoyed working her own patch of garden as a child, and thus gained much working knowledge of plants by hands-on involvement. Jekyll grew up with a strong sense of place for this region, and her deep attachment would later contribute much to her personal involvement in gardening.

Jekyll's first official movement toward a life in the arts began at the Kensington School of Art in London in 1861. She was able to broaden her educational perspectives and diversify her gardening background through study trips abroad to Switzerland, Italy, Greece, Spain, and North Africa. In 1865, she made the acquaintance of John Ruskin, whose ideas and books such as *The Stones of Venice* were *de rigueur* for progressively minded art students. Thus imbued with his anti-machine sentiments and the pursuit of beauty in natural forms, she met another of his students, William Morris, and eventually most other members of his circle. Morris would prove to be a profound influence on her. For Jekyll, it would prove to be a fortuitous time to be young, artistic, moderately well-off, and progressively minded enough to make the most of her connections. Just as it literally got off the ground, she became an active participant in the Arts and Crafts Movement.

It was first as a fine artist, and then as a craftsperson, that Jekyll's talents took form. She identified completely with the idea of fusing art and craftwork with daily life, and found it a compelling pursuit. With a zeal matched by few, she excelled in just about every craft undertaking she attempted; among her skills were those of fine metalwork, embroidery and tapestry, and woodworking (including carving and inlay). Because she was a woman, her status as a craftsperson remained officially that of an amateur, although she received some choice commissions from some of the most prominent and influential clientele in England. By the late 1860s, her parents' home had been relocated to Wargrave in Berkshire, and she was acutely homesick for her childhood home in Surrey. Nevertheless, she created a garden in Berkshire, and avidly continued to nurture that interest and skill.

By the mid-1870s, Jekyll's life altered its course. During years of intense, close-up work with her painting and myriad craft pursuits, she also began to experience a growing myopia. While she did not become blind, she began to use her energies in new pursuits. With characteristic aplomb she slipped quite readily into writing about a subject already dear to her heart—that of gardening. Her first opportunity came by way of William Robinson, whom she first met in 1875 at the offices of *The Garden*, and within three years her writing career was officially launched with articles for that periodical. The growing popularity of gardening as a hobby for many middle-class people, and the success of Robinson's publications proved a fine support for Jekyll's new career as a garden writer and designer.

When the family decided to return to Surrey from Berkshire, after her father died in 1876, Jekyll was back on her beloved turf for good. In designing and implementing her own gardening ideas at their new home, Munstead House, she used the ensuing tasks as basic material for her writing projects. By 1883, she had acquired fifteen acres of neighboring land on which to build a house of her own,

and while planning its construction, she began work on its garden.

Jekyll and Lutyens: The Garden and House Collaboration

Despite the absence of any house for almost fifteen years, Jekyll's own garden was gracefully evolving. In 1889, another turning point in her life occurred when she met a young architect named Edwin Lutyens (pronounced "Lutchenz," 1869–1944), who became the designer of her house, Munstead Wood, and her collaborator on some of the greatest houses and gardens of the Arts and Crafts period in England. That Lutyens was also from Surrey and had a great sensitivity to its vernacular architecture was certainly an enhancement to their initial connection, successful business partnership, and long friendship. Lutyens's career ranks high among the later generation of English Arts and Crafts architects. Most of his elegantly original designs recall historical influences but are filled with freshness and originality. He sometimes applied some of his legendary ingenuity into the design of furniture and accessories for his projects.

The partnership of Jekyll and Lutyens was a perfectly balanced combination of their skills. The young architect delighted in Jekyll's humor and down-to-earth qualities; they seldom had any disagreements. Her social connections were sources of excellent referrals for Lutyens' architectural commissons; between 1893 and 1912 they managed to create seventy gardens together. During the last several years of this period, however, their projects were increasingly characterized by movement away from the Arts and Crafts influence and toward that of the Classical Revival.

Not all of their projects were for new houses, and some of their most interesting work involved additions to existing properties. Among these are Hestercombe (1904–1908) in Somerset, where an existing, undistinguished house was transformed into something extraordinary by a new, spectacularly realized garden scheme, and Folly Farm (1906–1912) in Berkshire, where sympathetic additions and a garden were added, in two phases, to a much older farmhouse. Both were included in *Houses and Gardens*, a 1913 book authored by Lutyens and published by *Country Life* magazine.

Possibly their most significant collaboration occurred in 1901 for the design of The Deanery, a stunning ensemble of house and garden built at Sonning in Berkshire. Considered a masterpiece of harmony and restraint, it showcases the talents of both partners at their best; virtually every design concept dear to Jekyll's heart was fully

St. Francis Court, Pasadena, Cal.

11. Postcard showing St. Francis Court, Pasadena, California (1913). One of the earliest-known bungalow courts, dating to 1909, it was designed by architect Sylvanus Marston with a central driveway, an indication of the emerging importance of the automobile that would greatly affect Southern California's development. Seasonal stays by visitors from colder climates had created a demand for affordable rental properties, and bungalow courts proved to be a popular solution. Most bungalow courts had virtually identical houses, but each of the eleven units in St. Francis Court was built to a different design. When its site was redeveloped for commercial use, some of the St. Francis Court bungalows escaped demolition and were relocated elsewhere in town. (For another view see *The Bungalow*, fig. 26.)

12. Postcard showing "A Rose-Embowered Bungalow, California" (1918). Appearing to be more vegetation than house, this bungalow takes the widely recommended use of climbing vines to an extreme. Beneath the open pergola-type roof of its front porch are large potted plants. Many owners of new bungalows were eager to make their homes look well-established, and California's climate with its year-round growing season helped them speed up the process. More to be trusted as documents of period architecture than of gardens, the details of postcard photographs could be altered during the coloring process. Starting with a black and white print, the artists applying the color often invented hues for the flowers (or added them, where they didn't exist) for a showy effect. Despite this, postcards still tell us much about how many bungalows were originally landscaped. Because so many could thrive there, exotic plants had long been imported to California; recognizable at the left is a Norfolk Island Pine *(Araucaria excelsa)*, originally from Australia.

13385   A ROSE EMBOWERED BUNGALOW, CALIFORNIA   COPR. DETROIT PUBLISHING CO.

realized there. The Deanery was built for Edward Hudson, a friend of Jekyll's, who was also the publisher of *Country Life*. In Hudson the partners had a key client, who was enthusiastic about their work and interested in promoting it through coverage in his increasingly important periodical.

It is interesting to note that there were also three American gardens among Jekyll's commissions: the first was for Elmhurst (1914), near Cincinnati, Ohio, followed by Cotswold Cottage (1925) in Greenwich, Connecticut, and Old Glebe House (1926) in Woodbury, Connecticut.

The Legacy of Jekyll

Reflecting the social-reform aspect of the Arts and Crafts Movement, Jekyll, with her upbringing and liberal education, was a socially progressive feminist. She had a long, active interest and involvement in the Women's Suffrage movement, and was also influential in establishing opportunities for women to receive professional training as gardeners.

Of all her contributions to garden design and practice, the one most often cited is her inventive use of color in the mixed border. Inspiration for her painterly approach to color in a garden has been traced to her art background and also to her admiration of British painter J.M.W. Turner (1775–1851). Completely unlike any other painter of his time, his style was dramatically abstract. Turner combined colors in a sweepingly complex yet seemingly natural way that fascinated Jekyll. In an effort to learn his technique, she is known to have spent days at the National Gallery copying his work.

These carefully honed color skills were mirrored in her handling of the flower border. Inspired by cottage-garden borders, she refined it into a calculated art form. In Jekyll's capable hands, despite the appearance of almost naturalistic casualness, little was accidental. For predictable effects, she constructed the "bones" of her borders with a palette of hardy perennials, biennials, bulbs, and tuberous plants. Arranged to avoid the appearance of rigid order, her borders were one component of a carefully conceived plan. Her diagrams for borders resemble patchwork "crazy quilts," except that the patches are rounded, elongated drifts or swaths of color in planted areas that overlap and intertwine with each other in what appear to be completely accidental relationships. Jekyll was a master at balancing color so that it dazzled, but didn't overwhelm; she also knew exactly how to mix and match certain plantings to achieve the greatest length of blooming time for her borders.

Her own garden at Munstead Wood was a veritable laboratory for testing her ideas, such as camouflaging the declining foliage of early-flowering delphiniums with the vines of a later-flowering clematis. Such inventive solutions to common planting problems seem to be based on equal parts of common sense and keen imagination, and are well worth emulating. Although gardens tend to be difficult to restore (less so for their architectural elements), an ongoing restoration of Jekyll's own garden has been undertaken. Among her extant works, it remains the most revealing of her personality and approach to gardening. Inasmuch as Jekyll was the author of over two thousand articles and thirteen books, it is a lasting benefit for today's gardening enthusiast that many of Jekyll's books have been reissued and are currently in print.

Jekyll worked on garden designs for about 250 different locations, so the total number of her existing drawings approaches two thousand. Fortunately, most of this extraordinary archive has been preserved and is now at the School of Environmental Design of the University of California, Berkeley. It was bequeathed to the school by the noted American landscape architect Beatrix Farrand (1872–1959), who purchased the drawings in 1948. Known as the Reef Collection, it was named after Farrand's summer home in Maine.

Like Jekyll, Farrand had a refined family background; she was a favorite niece of famed American novelist Edith Wharton. Her aunt shared her love of gardens (among Wharton's writings is the *Italian Villas and Gardens* of 1903, illustrated by Maxfield Parrish), and encouraged Farrand's interest in them. Traveling, Farrand visited Jekyll at Munstead Wood, and later she credited the success of her own work to Jekyll's influence. Like her mentor, she spent much of her career designing the gardens of large estates. Another example of a successful woman in a male-dominated profession, she was one of the founding members of the American Society of Landscape Designers. Among Farrand's best known projects are the famous gardens of Dumbarton Oaks in Washington, D.C., and the campus plans for Yale University, New Haven, Connecticut, and Princeton University, Princeton, New Jersey.

Other British Arts and Crafts architects also made gardens an integral part of their residential projects. Inspired by Morris and Webb, they shared a common interest in adapting the local building traditions into their projects, although each had a distinctive style. The best known are: Charles Rennie Mackintosh (1868–1928), M.H. Baillie Scott (1865–1945), and C.F.A. Voysey (1857–1941). Like Lutyens, most of their commissions were for large homes and their gardens. Despite a generous size, many of these homes have a remarkably inviting and almost cozy quality that extends into the living spaces of their gardens.

13. Garden plan for Bungalow No. 104 (1914). Many bungalows were built on narrow lots, which limited most of their landscaping impact to the front and rear yards. One of four plans offered for a 35-foot-wide lot, the lack of a driveway next to this house suggests that a service alley might be at the rear. Befitting a corner location, the wrap-around porch would also help add to a feeling of space in the front yard. Walkways from the street and down the side yard avoid any straight lines, thus helping to vary the shapes of planting beds. Across the rear property line is a utility zone formed by a shed (or garage) and space for a vegetable garden. An illusion of greater depth and width at the back of the house is reinforced by the curving paths of stepping stones and meandering outlines of planted areas. A covered pavilion ("P") or outdoor room is placed off-center and tucked behind a clump of trees and boulders. Planting lists for each plan in this book were available by mail order for a small charge. This plan and the ones depicted in figures 16 and 23 are taken from *California Gardens,* written and published in 1914 by Eugene O. Murmann.

PLAN NO. 3
Size of Lot 35'x135'

Sources of the American Arts and Crafts Garden

During the first half of the nineteenth century, much of North America was unsettled virgin wilderness with many of its centuries-old Native American cultures substantially intact. With the subsequent settling of the continent, rugged simplicity and "living off the land" became hallowed traditions. The log cabin, an icon of pioneering courage and self-sufficiency, was adopted by the American Arts and Crafts Movement as a symbol of vernacular architecture and became popular for vacation houses because of its rustic informality.

Most American craft traditions were utilitarian in nature and not initially admired for their aesthetic beauty. The first of these crafts to be reassessed were the basketry, pottery, and textiles of the Native American cultures, which would become avidly admired, collected, and sometimes emulated during the Arts and Crafts period.

Success has long been a respected American cultural phenomenon. For many, their success once achieved, issues of fashion were defined by emulating the pretensions and tastes of England and other European cultures. By the Victorian era, many had lost complete sight of the inspiration and beauty to be found in nature. Toward the late 1800s, one reaction to Victorian tastes and conventions was the rustic-design sensibility, an almost aggressively informal influence that had reappeared in America. In contrast with the so-called rustic cast-iron novelty furniture that had already appeared in mid-century England and America, these later pieces were handcrafted from wood. Popularly associated with summer camps and cottages and still considered a novelty, it was dubbed Adirondack style.

Using plain lumber, logs (with bark intact), or irregular tree branches in its construction, the Adirondack style was applied to both furniture and architecture. The style found its way into gardens as furniture, fences, or arbors to support vines. The architectural style of vacation houses in the Adirondacks and other resort areas subsequently influenced bungalow design. The significance of America's rustic styles is that they unabashedly expressed our own culture.

After trade was reopened with Japan by the mid-1850s, it became a design source from which Americans would borrow quite freely, and it also had a major impact on our garden designs, plants, and practices. Many were first exposed to the art and export products of Japan at various World's Fairs, such as the 1876 Centennial Exposition in Philadelphia. Even more influential, particularly on such architects as Frank Lloyd Wright and the Greene brothers, was the Japanese exhibit at the 1893 World's Columbian Exposition in Chicago, for it featured a half-scale reconstruction of the Phoenix Hall of the Byodo-in Temple at Uji, near Kyoto in Japan. This exotic building provided an impressive example of a traditional Japanese timber-frame building. A smaller-scale event in 1894 was San Francisco's Midwinter Fair that featured the stunning Japanese Tea Garden, which to many was—and still remains—an artistic and horticultural revelation.

Thus an American fashion for Japanese gardens was born, especially among those who could afford to indulge their aesthetic fantasies. Working their magic on even the most compact outdoor spaces, "Japanese gardens" appeared across the country: Glimpses through exotic gateways revealed lily ponds of irregular form, ringed by imported plants and trees, and watched over by stone lanterns. The absorption of Japan into the design sensibilities of the American Arts and Crafts Movement would be profound.

Despite its mid-nineteenth century emergence in England, outward evidence of the Arts and Crafts Movement was slow to appear in America. Those who first became aware of the new aesthetic were well-traveled or informed craftspeople or others with connections to the fields of architecture and interior design. Toward the end of the century, America had emerged as a leading force in modern architecture, especially for large commercial-building projects—particularly, early skyscrapers. In some architectural trade journals the latest residential designs were showcased and frequently included the residential work of such English architects as Lutyens, Voysey, and Baillie Scott. Gardens for these projects were sometimes illustrated in plan drawings, and the work of these architects had some influence on their American colleagues, but most professionally "designed" gardens done here were for large estates, and their formal features were often adapted from those of Italian Renaissance villas.

When people became fully aware of the Arts and Crafts style, it was considered modest and unpretentious, and independent-minded, middle-class Americans could identify with its ideas of improving daily life through an artistic, craft-related pursuit—a therapeutic hobby. For some, this meant working at a craft, such as with wood, metal, or textiles, but for many Americans, then as now, gardening became their passion.

Frank Lloyd Wright (1867–1959) emerged as a uniquely American force during this period and soon became internationally known for his innovative Prairie Style houses. Despite their modernity, the houses showed the influence of English Arts and Crafts in the central placement of fireplaces ("hearth and home"). Wright's debt to Japan was also evident in the simple linear detailing of the architecture and the use of natural materials for finishes and furniture. A calculated relationship of the house to its site was a major part of his organic-design philosophy. He broke his

A Typical Bungalow in California.

14. Postcard showing "A Typical Bungalow in California" (1916). The immaturity of this landscaping scheme betrays the newness of the house, but it probably didn't stay that way for long in the California climate. The plants appear to be a combination of desert *(yucca)* and subtropical *(palm and poinsettia)*. Suspended from the exposed trusswork timbers in the open gable of the front porch is an array of hanging plants that helps to shield the sitting area from the street. The masonry of this bungalow's chimney and front porch are in the so-called "Peanut-Brittle style," a variation of Craftsman, which has irregular courses of dark clinker brick combined with smooth, light-colored river rock to give natural-looking texture.

A California Bungalow in Winter.

15. Postcard showing "A California Bungalow in Winter" (c.1915) . A particularly delightful way to merge a bungalow's interior rooms with its outdoor garden spaces was to position them around an open courtyard. This example shows how this could be accomplished on a modest scale and still be effective. Visitors pass through an open-columned porch into a roofless outdoor room containing blooming plants and perhaps centered on a splashing fountain or lily pond. Although inspired by early California haciendas, not all courtyard bungalows were of the Spanish or Mission Revival styles; the columns of this example suggest the Colonial Revival influence combined with Craftsman-style windows and low-slung proportions.

living spaces out of the traditional "box" structure of the house and spilled them into the garden. His widely published work was recognized as an important contribution to the field of architecture, and it also influenced bungalow design.

Bungalows that most exemplify the Arts and Crafts aesthetic fuse house to garden in a natural setting, and make extensive use of simple, natural building materials, configured to express their assembly outwardly. These are characteristic of what was soon to become widely known as the Craftsman style. Eschewing the excessive, fretsawed or machine-milled ornament of their Victorian predecessors, these designs highlighted the beauty of wood joinery, often reflecting a Japanese influence in their exposed timber framing. The ideal of preserving the integrity of construction was guided by the same aesthetic that produced items of such understated richness in the Movement's handcrafted decorative arts for the interior.

With the public's growing awareness of the importance of harmony in the relationship of a house to its landscape, the bungalow and its garden became emblematic of a modern, artistic American home. Reflecting a sensible practicality combined with convenience, these modest homes perfectly suited their moment at the start of a new century. With a wealth of new house plans that were widely promoted, *bungalow* quickly became an American household word. While it combined the best of aesthetics and practicality, perhaps the greatest appeal of the bungalow was affordability; it was a dream within reach of the average American family.

The bungalow's appeal marked it as a new housing phenomenon. Mostly radiating from the West, and especially associated with its early popularity in California, bungalows were quick to appear across the nation wherever new housing was needed. Their popularity was strengthened by far-reaching exposure in design-advice books and periodicals, such as *House and Garden*, *House Beautiful*, and *Ladies' Home Journal*. These mainstream magazines published many articles about bungalows and their gardens along with their usual coverage of larger, more expensive homes. It was Gustav Stickley who, in his own magazine *The Craftsman*, was responsible for coining the term *Craftsman* as the latest housing style.

Unlike anything seen before, the popularity of bungalows made them a favorite house style for builders and real-estate developers responsible for constructing many large tracts in rapidly developing areas, especially in California and Florida. For more choices, many homebuyers shopped for their dream house in widely distributed catalogs, sometimes called plan books, which offered complete sets of builder-ready working drawings at minimal cost. Others preferred the ultimate convenience of having a "ready-cut" (prefabricated) house shipped in pieces to be assembled on site. This concept was first widely marketed nationwide by Sears, Roebuck and Company beginning in 1909, and their success soon encouraged others to follow suit.

Gustav Stickley and the Craftsman Empire

Gustav Stickley (1858–1942) was the person most responsible for delivering the Movement's design, if not its philosophy, to America on a major scale, including promoting it as an influence on gardens. Stickley had already been involved in furniture-making before he traveled to England in 1898, where he met Voysey and Ashbee, and became immersed in Arts and Crafts design and philosophy.

Transformed by the experience, he decided that Americans would also enjoy the straightforward, no-nonsense design approach to furniture that had impressed him. Stickley believed its potential for the American market lay in his promotion of the Arts and Crafts Movement's philosophy and design.

In addition to being creative and artistically minded, Stickley was determined to become a businessman. He decided that a magazine would be an ideal vehicle for spreading his ideas and expanding his client base for furniture sales. Called *The Craftsman*, it was published between 1901 and 1916, and it was responsible for many Americans learning about William Morris and the Arts and Crafts Movement. While he began *The Craftsman* with a more politically motivated, pro-Socialist slant directly inspired by Morris, Stickley soon made it less controversial for his audience. Stickley's increasingly personal version of the Movement's philosophy enabled him to claim it as his own, so everything he sold was marketed under his self-styled Craftsman label.

After a 1904 trip to California, he saw potential in the bungalow's combination of simplicity and sophistication, and agreed that the importance of gardens to the bungalow aesthetic was appealing and timely. Through Stickley's guidance his growing readership soon considered bungalows as an ideal Craftsman home.

Stickley was impressed with the California work of Charles Greene and Henry Greene and the way in which Japan had influenced their ideas. Examples of their homes, outdoor living spaces, and details were enthusiastically presented in *The Craftsman*. The two architects in turn admired Stickley's work, and they specified his furniture for some projects that lacked the budget (or client approval) to support commissions for their own furniture designs.

Stickley banked his success on the changing tastes of Americans, most of whom were increasingly receptive to

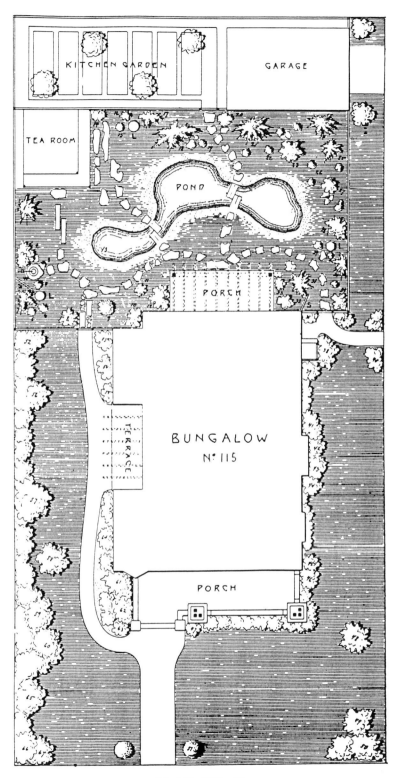

PLAN NO. 39
Size of Corner Lot 75'x150'

16. Garden plan for Bungalow No. 115 (1914). Designed for a 75-foot-wide by 150-foot-deep corner lot, this plan has a garage and a secondary entrance to the house on the right (or street) side. Compared with figure 13, the lot is only fifteen feet longer, but its width has been more than doubled, allowing the side-yard areas to be of greater use. Because the right side comprises part of the home's "street identity," it should be landscaped in close relationship to the front side, as both will be seen together. The side yard at the left is overlooked by a recessed terrace that faces a private garden area screened from any direct street view. To screen the neighboring house, a privacy wall created by shrubbery and trees is planted along the property line. The most interesting part of the plan is in the enclosed rear yard behind the house. Inspired by a Japanese tea garden, it is treated as a separate world, and intentionally doesn't interact with the other garden areas. A large, free-form pond with two rustic stone bridges is the focal point, interlaced with stepping-stone paths. Japanese-style garden accents include stone lanterns ("L"), a stone well ("W"), and wooden screens ("S"), which are situated among artfully arranged groupings of rocks and plants, and overlooked by a wisteria-covered porch with an open-beam pergola roof. Conserving precious space, a tearoom abuts the property line at an inside corner to form a secluded retreat. Behind it, aligned with the side and matching the width of the garage, a kitchen garden extends across the remaining rear area of the property.

moving beyond the Victorian age. Bungalows were featured prominently in his magazine, together with larger Craftsman homes. Stickley promoted the versatility of bungalows by designing and selling house plans, and suggested that many were appropriate as either vacation or affordable year-round houses. He also regularly published articles about Craftsman gardens and garden-related subjects. Preaching the importance of a garden's relationship to the house, the magazine encouraged the use of outdoor living spaces as an indispensable part of healthful family living.

Stickley became intrigued with the idea of creating a rural community of craftspeople working in harmony and living in supportive proximity, and wrote about this concept in *The Craftsman*. He envisioned this community as a mostly self-sufficient group, whose members would be responsible for growing their own food and raising their own livestock. This was reminiscent of other turn-of-the-century American Arts and Crafts communities, such as the Rose Valley Association founded in 1901 by William Price outside of Philadelphia, and Byrdcliffe founded in 1902 by Ralph Whitehead (a transplanted Englishman) at Woodstock, New York. As was true of the English craft groups inspired by Morris, most American community ventures produced beautiful objects and furnishings but were relatively short-lived because of the familiar conflict of idealism with reality.

Although Stickley's own dream of such a utopian community never took form, it probably was a factor in his decision to purchase 650 picturesque country acres in 1907, now located in the township of Parsippany-Troy Hills, near Morristown, New Jersey. He had transformed his idea of a rural community into one for a boys' school, where vocational training in various craft skills would be administered by master craftsmen. The curriculum planned for Craftsman Farms was to have the healthful counterbalance of a hands-on training program for farming skills to help staff the site as a functioning farm. By 1909, the farm-school idea hadn't been realized, but Stickley had built several small bungalows on the property. Other auxiliary structures were constructed by 1912, including a hen house, a dairy barn, and a horse stable.

A large house constructed of logs and boulders was completed by 1911. In November of that year, Stickley praised his new creation in *The Craftsman*, recounting America's nostalgic associations with log cabins and pointing out their parallels in Japanese architecture. Originally planned as the central Club House of Craftsman Farms, this building served instead as Stickley's own home for several years. Sited on its grassy rise in a wooded landscape, the house overlooks a small pond, and early photographs show a harmonious blend of planting beds and existing foliage.

Plans are now underway for restoration of the original landscaping.

The concept of Craftsman Farms as a functioning school was never realized, but today it is open to the public as the Stickley Museum after impressive restoration. Home of the Craftsman Farms Foundation, the site is important in promoting awareness and on-going study of Stickley and the American Arts and Crafts Movement.

Spread too thin by his other business obligations, Stickley's attention to the country property was overshadowed in 1913, when he leased a twelve-story office building in nearby New York City to house company showrooms and business headquarters. By 1915, Stickley's increasing financial difficulties had led him to file bankruptcy. His magazine ceased publication in 1916 and, in 1917, when Craftsman Farms was sold to help pay off his creditors, he retreated with his family to Syracuse, New York.

Elbert Hubbard and the Roycroft Community

Another major American force in the marketing of Arts and Crafts ideas and furnishings, Elbert Hubbard achieved remarkable success. This part of his life occurred after he had retired from a twenty-year career with the Larkin Company of Buffalo, New York, a manufacturer of soaps and toiletries. The Larkin Company building was one of the masterful creations in the early career of Frank Lloyd Wright. Like Stickley, Hubbard had traveled to England, where achievements of the Arts and Crafts Movement impressed him—particularly William Morris's Kelmscott Press at Hammersmith. He founded the Roycroft community in East Aurora, New York, and the Roycroft Press began to publish his periodical, *The Philistine*, in 1895. Other crafts, notably metalwork and furniture, soon followed. Bringing considerable business acumen to his new endeavor, Hubbard kept a close watch over the work and budget. Drawing on successful sales techniques of his days with the Larkin Company, a considerable amount of Roycroft sales was also done by mail order.

The Roycroft community attracted many skilled craftspeople drawn there by the activity and camaraderie of a lively and vital working environment, where it was actually possible to make a living. By 1900, there were 175 people working there; at its peak, the total work force exceeded 500. Hubbard and the Roycrofters came closest to achieving the ideal of a working Arts and Crafts community.

In addition to the national lecture circuit pursued by Hubbard, there were multiple annual lecture events locally staged by the Roycrofters, which drew many attendees and prospective clients. As the needs of the working

17. Detail of a bungalow porch in Berkeley, California (1905). This spectacular wisteria-draped front porch makes clear why it was one of the most popular flowering vines of the early twentieth century. Built in the Scenic Park Tract development in the Berkeley hills, the house would probably have received the approval of the city's Hillside Club, which promoted landscaping as the best way to blend new houses into their natural surroundings.

18. Bungalow streetscape in Portland, Oregon (c.1920). The homes on this street are set on a slight rise that gives a pleasant feeling of separation from the sidewalk. Framed with low retaining walls of small boulders, the front yard of the bungalow on the right contains a bed of mixed perennials. The varied textures and colors of their foliage helps keep this garden interesting regardless of what is or isn't in bloom. A novel effect is created by a mass of white clematis twining up the trunk of a large maple tree, and climbing roses are trained up small wooden trellises set against the house. Seen through the branches of a pink dogwood at left, the Craftsman-style informality of the bungalow next door contrasts with the more traditional Colonial Revival details of the home on the right—classical porch columns, narrow clapboard siding, and triangular gable pediments.

community grew, its location near the center of the small village of East Aurora developed into an inviting campus of picturesque buildings, loosely modeled on English medieval and Tudor styles. To accommodate the influx of Roycroft visitors, in 1903 Hubbard had the Print Shop converted into the Roycroft Inn. Over time, Hubbard continued to incorporate available adjacent land and also purchased nearby housing to accommodate workers and their families.

Hubbard's leadership abruptly ceased in 1915, for he and his wife, Alice, were lost in the sinking of the liner *Lusitania* by a German submarine. The Roycroft community carried on under the direction of Hubbard's eldest son, Elbert II ("Bert"), but it would never again achieve the prominence and success it had during his father's tenure. Eventually, changing public tastes and financial instability suffered during the Great Depression led to the end of all Roycroft business activity in 1938.

Unlike Stickley, Hubbard and the Roycrofters were not involved in creating or selling the design of architecture or gardens as a routine part of their business. However, their interest in gardening is implied by an advertisement for Vigoro plant food that appeared in the February 1931 issue of *Better Homes and Gardens*. The caption for a garden view of the Roycroft campus says "See what Vigoro has done for the Roycrofters, East Aurora, New York," and is accompanied by a brief testimonial quote by Elbert Hubbard II, that "Vigoro has had a marked influence on all our growing things." The choice of the Roycrofters for such a product endorsement in a national magazine is a good indication of their high visibility with the general public.

A visit to East Aurora today shows a number of Craftsman-style bungalows dating from the early Roycroft period that are situated close to the campus. One of them now houses the Elbert Hubbard Museum and has a garden with some original period features and plantings. The area in and around the campus has been revitalized by an active, ongoing revival of the local Arts and Crafts community, spearheaded by the efforts of the Foundation for the Study of the Arts and Crafts Movement at Roycroft. A remarkable number of the campus buildings has survived, and most have been reclaimed for new uses. The former Blacksmith (and subsequent Copper) Shop now houses the Roycroft Shops, and the former Chapel is now the City Hall of East Aurora. After an extensive restoration, the Roycroft Inn was reopened for business in 1995 in time for the community's centennial.

California and the Arts and Crafts Garden

The region most often associated with the bungalow's popularity is California, which strongly influenced the plan-

ning of indoor-outdoor living. Even as bungalows spread to less-benign climates, the garden remained an integral part of a bungalow plan. No matter where they were built, gardens overlooked by roomy open porches and pergola-covered patios were a constant feature. In or out of California, the popularity of gardening helped seal the success of the bungalow, and not surprisingly, the areas of America with the mildest climates were also major sites of bungalow development.

The increasing interest in the specialness of California has often been attributed to the wide popularity of Helen Hunt Jackson's novel *Ramona*. First published in 1884, the book painted a vivid picture of California frontier life in the context of both its Spanish Colonial and Native American cultures. Despite the fact that it is fiction, the "true" setting of the novel became subject to much public speculation. Because its author was known to have visited there in 1882, many came to believe it was Rancho Guajome in San Diego county, a fine surviving example of Anglo-Hispanic domestic architecture. Constructed of adobe bricks, it was originally built by Cave Johnson Couts in 1852–1853 on a Mexican land grant near the Mission of San Luis Rey. In 1902 the original builder's brother offered guided tours of the property for those caught up in its legend. Now restored, Rancho Guajome remains one of the most important, revealing, and evocative historic sites in California.

Encouraged by the popularity of *Ramona*, public interest in the forms of early California architecture and gardens it described was significantly increased. The plans of so-called hacienda houses, like the one at Rancho Guajome, were typically only one room deep and arranged in a square or U-shape to enclose an inner courtyard. This was ringed inside by a shady covered veranda that functioned both as outdoor sitting areas and as circulation between some otherwise unconnected rooms.

The garden that was protected within the courtyard formed a verdant oasis in dusty, arid surroundings. The arrangement of interior and outdoor spaces around what was essentially a large outdoor room encouraged almost continuous interaction with the garden. In 1868, a visitor to Rancho Guajome described its inner courtyard as planted with oleander, orange, and lemon trees, and that its overhanging veranda was festooned with vining passion flowers. Growing in an orchard next to the house were more lemons and oranges, as well as figs, olives, pomegranates, persimmons, and black walnuts.

These homes employed a simple and straightforward use of natural materials that successfully fulfilled the functional needs of their occupants. As classic examples of vernacular architecture, along with the earlier Mission Church compounds, these adobe buildings became subject to much admiration and as valid to Arts and Crafts sensibilities as the stone farm cottages of England, or

19. Bungalow front porch, Pasadena, California (c.1915). This welcoming front porch is framed by columns faced with river rock and wreathed by foliage that helps to meld it with the garden edged with river rock. Comfortably outfitted with a large suspended swing and deep cushions, the porch makes a picture-perfect image of bungalow living. Created in simplified Craftsman style, the house features two prominent front-facing gables, each of which contains airy lattice grids backed by screens that help keep the attic ventilated.

20. Garden steps, Short Hills, New Jersey (1907). Creating graceful circulation between different garden levels can be a challenge, but it can also be among the most satisfying of its architectural elements. This original example, designed by architects Albro & Lindeberg, connects a broad, sunny lawn area to a more secluded shady space that overlooks a neighboring pond. There is a relaxed sense of formality in these rising arcs of steps that is always inviting, for nature still dominates this elegant composition. (For another view see fig. 253.)

22. View of a pond, terrace, and garden, southern Rhode Island (1931–1932). This stunning garden design respects the natural terrain of the site and incorporates some of the elements into the formal scheme. Left of center at the far end is a group of granite boulders that are part of the wooded landscape surrounding this garden. In the best English Arts and Crafts country house style, this sweeping vista is viewed from an open terrace outside the living room. The handsome terrace arc, paved with irregular flagstones, seems to float above a reflecting pool. A small circular pond, which is fully recessed into the lawn, forms a counterbalance at the far end. The sweeping length of the low stone walls and perennial beds are seen here to their best advantage. Despite its elegant organization, the most dramatic effects seen here are those provided by nature, which is certainly a good rule of thumb for almost any garden. (For other views see figs. 21, 97, 121, 137, 185.)

21. (Opposite) Detail of a mixed-planting bed, southern Rhode Island (1931–1932). The delightfully resolved order of this bed of mixed hardy perennials suggests that its gardener is familiar with English Arts and Crafts traditions. There is a clear division between the orderly low hedge and groomed lawn at the right, and the scintillating abundance of iris and peonies that leads into the trees and shrubs at the left. While always subordinate to the plantings, there are some handsome architectural bones here, which are also indebted to the best of the English Arts and Crafts garden style. Organized as logical extensions of the house (partially seen at the upper right), low fieldstone walls anchor the long borders and rise to form square pedestals supporting terra-cotta urns as they change level to meet the house, designed by architect George Howe and built with the same fieldstone.

25

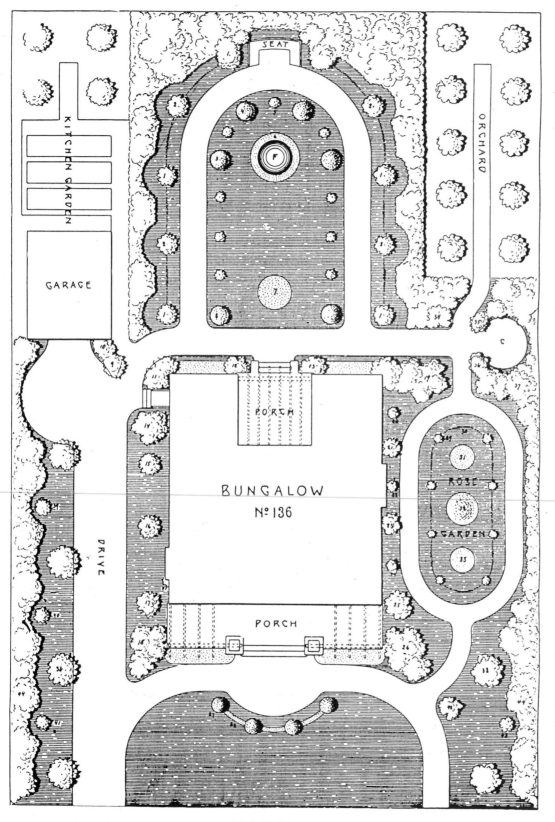

SEAT

KITCHEN GARDEN

GARAGE

ORCHARD

F

PORCH

DRIVE

BUNGALOW
N° 136

ROSE GARDEN

C

PORCH

PLAN NO. 44
Size of Lot 100'x150'

23. Garden plan for Bungalow No. 136 (1914). With a generous lot size 100 feet wide by 150 feet deep, this plan has been quite formally organized, thus reflecting some of the collaborative designs made by Edwin Lutyens and Gertrude Jekyll in England. English Arts and Crafts architects tended to favor a logical, structured approach in developing a sequence of garden spaces; they preferred artistic expression through traditional, unpretentious building materials and sensitive placement and choice of plantings. English Arts and Crafts garden design avoided attempts at recreating the calculated sense of informality of Japanese gardens that was so willingly adopted in America. In this plan, the central placement of the bungalow and curving arc of driveway leading to the front porch provides a feeling of order and symmetry. While such balance guides the plan's organization throughout, it is maintained without slavish use, and is most noticeable in the layout of the rear yard. A strong linear axis runs through the center of the house and rear yard, which ends at the seat at the far end of the lot. Parallel walkways flank the central lawn area that has a round fountain and round planting bed aligned through the center. This handsome vista is surveyed from a deeply recessed porch or outdoor room at the back of the house. A secondary cross-axis connects the service areas of garage and kitchen garden with a circular seating area ("C") at the opposite side of the lot. This retreat is placed between a modest orchard concealed behind hedges like the other utility areas, and a formal oval rose garden. Throughout the plan, vegetation is used to soften hard edges and geometry.

26

24. Garden arch, Oregon City, Oregon. Nature sometimes allows the architectural elements of gardens to become almost indistinguishable. All traces of the underlying structure of this arch have been completely obliterated by a profusion of rhododendron, fern, and ivy, which is crowned by spectacular clematis. While gardeners are inclined to manicure their creations, it would almost be a sin to prune such natural beauty. The arch covers a pathway that leads up through a hillside garden to a 1910 Craftsman-style house overlooking the Willamette River. (For another view see fig. 133; also *Inside the Bungalow*, figs 35, 225.)

America's log cabins. Reinterpreted as the Mission Revival style, examples of its romanticized adaptations extended to many bungalows.

Another California influence, which was echoed in Arts and Crafts garden design across the country, was the idea of incorporating native plants in a designed landscape to create a more natural appearance. A well-known example is the garden of El Alisal, the Highland Park (now part of Los Angeles) home of Charles Fletcher Lummis. The courtyard of the house was built around a large sycamore and the name he gave to the house was taken from the tree's Spanish name. Built on an undeveloped tract of land dotted with native trees and plants, Lummis planned that the site surrounding the house should remain as untouched as possible. He wrote rhapsodically of the most visually arresting section, and about what occurred each spring—an open meadow stretching away from the house became a vivid carpet of wildflowers, which continued its blooming during a six- to ten-week period until the rainless summers of the region began. Highlighted by the deep orange-gold of California poppies (*Eschscholzia californica*), the tapestry-like effect was filled out by other wild flowers, that included California wild oats (*Avena fatua*), Spanish lily (*Brodiaea capitata*), owl clover (*Orthocarpus purpurascens*), silver tips (*Potentilla anserina*), and tidytips (*Layia platyglossa*).

With the help of local Isleta Indians, construction on El Alisal began in 1895. Lummis built it with boulders carefully selected from a nearby *arroyo* (creekbed), which were then combined in a rambling composition of extremely personal style. Intended to evoke broadly the early days of California, the house and its plan were highly eclectic, but had some hacienda-like and Mission Revival features. Its primary importance to the history of the Arts and Crafts garden is that it represents an early, ambitious attempt to blend a newly constructed American house into its natural landscape.

Lummis was a writer known for his colorful personality. He emerged from the East Coast as a Harvard graduate, but was determined to make his literary mark on the world in an unconventional way. His remarkable career was launched when he decided to walk from Cincinnati to Los Angeles and then write about his observations and experiences for the *Los Angeles Times*. Settling in Southern California, he became city editor of that paper and began to express his interest in the history of California and the West, especially in relation to its Indian, Spanish, and Mexican cultures. These interests resulted in his founding of the Southwest Museum, which exhibits the arts of Native Americans, and the California Landmarks Club, which started restoration efforts on the state's early missions.

Now open to the public as a house museum, the architecture of El Alisal is more intact than its original garden.

The large sycamore is gone and the area of the garden is much reduced in size and surrounded by subsequent development. It no longer includes the natural meadow that Lummis prized. Even in its fragmentary state, the landscape still evokes its natural past, and is cultivated with plantings that serve as examples of drought-tolerant gardening for the region.

If Lummis pioneered the idea of a natural meadow garden in California, Kate Sessions (1857–1940) tamed it and put it to work. Born in San Francisco, she was a noted horticulturist and landscape designer who made her home in the San Diego area. With a keen interest in plants adapted to the local climate, she also for many years operated a florist shop and a nursery that specialized in native plants. She was responsible for introducing many plants to the local marketplace, and almost singlehandedly transformed the landscape of San Diego. Through contracts with the city of San Diego, she supplied many of the *Cocos Plumosa* palms lining its streets. She worked on many local projects, including the city's famous Balboa Park, where a commemorative statue of her was erected in 1998. In addition to the gardens of many private homes, she also worked on the gardens of the Hotel Del Coronado.

Despite their popularity with many who moved to the area from wetter regions, Sessions discouraged having water-guzzling lawns in local landscaping schemes, and encouraged substituting a wide selection of plantings more compatible with the dry climate. Among these are the dramatically spiked forms of yucca and agave, still very much in evidence in the residential landscaping of San Diego today.

A good example of her approach was the garden Sessions designed in 1911 for the B.F. Chase house in San Diego in collaboration with the progressive and influential architect Irving Gill (1870-1936). In a logical and practical response to the region, she chose a variety of drought-tolerant plants for the hillside garden, and set them into a series of terraces formed by low retaining walls of local stone. Although she encouraged their use, not all of her plant choices were indigenous. The bougainvillea, banana, cotoneaster, eucalyptus, and Italian cypress she used were imported species, and would become extremely popular throughout the region.

Irving Gill began his career working in historic-revival styles, and had a strong feeling for natural materials and the Craftsman aesthetic. Sometimes considered proto-modern, Gill's later signature style interprets elements of the Mission Revival in an abstraction of its forms. He made dramatic use of white-painted stucco cubic volumes, rounded arches, and the strong shadows created by deeply recessed arcades. His residential projects also promoted outdoor living through the use of terraces, pergolas, courtyards, and walled gardens.

The subject of Arts and Crafts design in California has

25. Garden view with pergola and garage, Portland, Oregon (c.1920). The garden seen here shows how the general scheme seen in figures 22 and 23 can be successfully used on a smaller scale. It has the axial plan seen in many larger gardens and includes a change in level seen in the steps at the left. The medieval "half-timbered" element of the English Tudor Revival, which was especially popular in the Twenties, is seen in the garage at the rear of the lot. The pergola at the right, which is shrouded with vines, terminates the long view from the house and contains a bench-swing. Paving patterns vary from the interlocking marble rectangles in the straight path, to a crazy-quilt patchwork design in the circle surrounding the rosebush. (For another view see fig. 115.)

26. Rustic arbor with built-in seating, Los Angeles, California. Rustic architecture and furniture is usually associated with vacation homes and the Adirondack style, but it also enjoyed some popularity in turn-of-the-century gardens. The simplicity of its careful assembly of unpeeled logs and branches appealed to the American Arts and Crafts sensibility. This example of the style is a well-resolved balance of tasteful proportions that incorporates garden seating. Recently constructed in this garden of a house in the Windsor Square area, it also forms a portal for winding pathways that lead away from an open meadow garden (see fig. 27) to other outdoor sitting areas.

27. Meadow garden of native plants, Los Angeles, California. Created in the spirit of the natural meadow garden at El Alisal made by Charles Fletcher Lummis, part of this new garden of a 1912 house in the Windsor Square area uses only native California plants. Their seasonal responses to the Mediterranean climate recreate the same remarkable variety of effects found in natural landscapes of the region. The issues of aesthetics and practicality in this garden have been artfully blended. Although no drought-tolerant garden can outsmart nature, this garden beautifully blurs the distinction. In the far left corner, a garden shed has been built in the perimeter walls.

become almost synonymous with the architecture of Greene and Greene, a partnership of brothers Charles Sumner Greene (1868–1957) and Henry Mather Greene (1870–1954). This book's eighth chapter highlights the gardens of several of their projects.

Also noteworthy is the work of Bay Area architect Bernard Maybeck (1862–1957), who created some of the finest Arts and Crafts homes in California, characterized by shingled or board-and-batten walls, and simple forms derived from such styles as English Tudor and Cottage, Swiss Chalet, and Craftsman. A confident and accomplished architect trained at the École des Beaux Arts in Paris, the broad range of his work demonstrated his skill with universal design principles. No matter what style he chose, he maintained a keen awareness of the importance of the connection of his houses to their sites and selected his choice of building materials accordingly.

Charles Keeler (1871–1937) was drawn into the world of architecture and design through his friendship with Maybeck, which resulted in his hiring Maybeck to design his new house and studio in the lower reaches of the Berkeley Hills in 1895. This was Maybeck's first residential commission, and it set the tone for many of his subsequent houses in the area. Keeler published a small but influential book in 1904 called *The Simple Home*. In it he emphasized many of the Hillside Club's ideals of architecture and landscape planning and echoed many thoughts derived from William Morris and associated with the Arts and Crafts Movement. He opposed the machine-age excesses of the Victorian age and envisioned the home as a place of spiritual sanctuary and renewal. The book expounded the beauty of natural materials as the most appropriate choices for homes and their interiors, and it was illustrated with photographs of Maybeck-designed houses (including Keeler's). In his chapter on gardens Keeler encouraged the careful adaptation of Japanese and Italian garden traditions and the judicious inclusion of exotic plants. Despite the fact that he was not trained in the subjects he discussed, he was never short of strong opinions, and his passionate and sometimes esoteric pronouncements reveal his remarkable mind.

While Maybeck and Keeler were adamant about houses not standing out in their landscape, they weren't necessarily partial to using just native plants, often characterized by gray-green foliage and limited blooming. They therefore promoted the use of plantings that were able to bloom profusely despite the season. An obvious problem with this approach is that it is water-intensive in a drought-prone area where resources for watering gardens can be limited. Nevertheless, many of the gardens that developed in the area were lush with imported plants and trees, and the pleasingly dense effect they created in a short period of time was very satisfying.

In the ensuing years, many of these gardens have failed because of subsequent neglect or drought, and some have been gradually replaced with plantings that are more suitable to the local climate. The bones of many of these hillside gardens are evident in their surviving retaining walls, which were created from the native stone. The art of rock gardening on hillsides was pioneered in California and remains a useful legacy of the Arts and Crafts period.

Approaching the Bungalow Garden Today

For many, the concerns about the restoration of their home's exterior or interior can seem relatively simple when compared to creating an appropriate garden scheme. The inexperienced gardener can take heart in the fact that one is bound by fewer rules in the realm of the garden than in tackling architectural restoration. What complicates this process with gardens is that many solutions are feasible, and it is likely that more than one might be considered appropriate. How to decide? Where to begin? Experienced gardeners know that such a problem can almost be liberating, for self-expression is one of gardening's greatest satisfactions.

Among the best solutions are garden designs that are original to the period. Always revealing, such documents of early twentieth-century taste are also rare. Because the next best thing to a period design is often an exact replacement, the first possibility to consider is making a replica based on the plans for or the remains of original gardens. Although early records or landscape drawings are uncommon for most bungalows, some gardens have enough parts of an original scheme remaining that it may be possible to reconstruct them, assisted by examining comparable examples of the period.

However, recreating the historic features of a bungalow garden with as much authenticity as possible is not necessarily the best approach. It can be aesthetically stifling for those who prefer a freer path of expression. Many recently designed garden elements are impressive examples of how creative expression can fuse successfully with historic sensibility.

Where nothing of consequence from the past remains, and the task is to create a completely new bungalow garden, fundamentals must first be decided. Some basic questions can guide the general direction of the planning before it gets underway. Is it a priority to express somehow the architectural style of the house? How closely should the design and plantings follow historic precedent?

Despite a bungalow's early association with the beauties of nature, many have been distanced from it in the ensuing years. The ongoing relationship of a house to its surroundings sometimes drastically changes from when it was

28. Desert landscaping, Borrego Springs, California (c.1950). A familiar feature of the regional landscape, the ocotillo *(Fouquieria splendens)* at the left grows in dramatically tall, spiky clumps. Growing low to the ground near its base is a prickly pear cactus *(Opuntia)*, the fruit of which is edible. Directly behind the ocotillo are some of Califonia's native fan palms *(Washingtonia robusta)*, which have been widely cultivated as ornamental trees since the nineteenth century. These grounds are part of a sprawling desert compound with indigenous landscaping designed by architect Cliff May. He is widely known as one of the major forces behind the development of the so-called ranch house that is sometimes considered the legacy of the bungalow. Combining various elements of the haciendas and low-slung wooden ranch houses of old California, May became famous for bringing a renewed freshness and style to the art of designing single-story homes. He began creating his versions of the ranch house in the 1930s, and few could match May's skill and sensitivity to the landscape.

built. Once-unspoiled adjoining property, which may have provided expansive views ("borrowed landscapes"), has probably succumbed to the relentless sprawl of real-estate development. Inside the property lines, what was perhaps once a personal-sized Eden may have been disfigured by ill-conceived asphalt paving, utility-pole easements, an out-of-place and oversize garage, or a mass of overgrown vegetation that inhibits garden views and accessibility.

Along with a renewal of interest in any historic house comes the need for more information about how to restore accurately or to remodel sympathetically. Bungalow devotees are no exception. Those who agree to tackle an old-house project are usually first smitten by its curb appeal, and therefore, initially most concerned with its exterior. Envisioning and implementing an appropriately designed garden setting can be one of the most immediate and dramatic improvements. Quite often such work can be done entirely by the homeowners. For this reason garden improvements tend to be somewhat kinder to the household budget than the required structural and cosmetic upgrades.

A fortunate few are able to locate historic documentation about their homes in the form of family photographs obtained from previous owners that can provide surprising amounts of information. Occasionally, such photographs include outside views that reveal how a porch was furnished, how parts of the garden were planted, where a per-

gola stood, or how a sundial or birdbath terminated a view. Another potential source of information would be to locate and interview any previous owners, occupants, or long-term neighbors. Sometimes surviving clues lie waiting for the observant eyes of a "domestic archaeologist." A forgotten path beneath overgrown shrubbery may be unearthed from years of accumulated debris and neglect by the clip of a blade or the turn of a trowel.

The now-vigorous bungalow-restoration movement has had a significant influence on new-home design and construction. If a new project is to adapt or interpret historic precedent successfully, it must include design professionals with a related educational background and working knowledge of the period. Much communicative dialogue between the new-house client and the project's architect, interior designer, landscape architect, and builder is essential for well-informed and timely design decisions. It is best to resolve as many questions as possible in the preliminary planning stages, so that the results will match or exceed the expectations.

As nature was a theme of central importance to the principles of the Arts and Crafts Movement, so too was the garden to bungalow living. It was housing that deliberately interacted with nature. Ensconced in its garden setting, the house became emblematic of an idealized, serene world of domestic bliss.

Garden Portraits

Views of Various Bungalow Gardens in Context with Their House and Its Style

One legacy of the Arts and Crafts Movement was a heightened awareness of the potential that gardens presented for individual artistic expression. Just as the exteriors and interiors of homes are perennial sources of fascination, so is our curiosity about how others have approached the design of their gardens and outdoor living spaces. The ongoing compulsion to observe and compare with others is simply part of a natural fact-finding mission to determine, confirm, and realize our own goals.

Developing a personal sense of style in the garden is something that takes practice. The most important ingredient is to have or develop an opinion, otherwise sound garden decisions cannot be made. As is true in other matters of personal taste, the precise reasons for likes and dislikes concerning gardens can't always be pinpointed; it is generally wise to trust gut-level instincts. It also helps to do some research, for it will lead to greater confidence and more informed decisions. A feeling for what is appropriate will emerge with greater clarity if it is supported by a basic background in historic or period-sensitive precedent. From planning to planting, the paybacks of gardening should be pleasures and not anxieties.

While considering the options, it can be particularly helpful to gain as much familiarity as possible with other comparable gardens. This can be done by viewing the gardens of neighbors and friends, or possibly by means of garden tours that are offered in many areas. Gardening periodicals and books can be helpful, but they cannot entirely supplant experiencing in person what others have accomplished. In defining aspirations for one's garden, appropriateness, as mentioned above, should be a main guide. Even modest gardens can challenge the most fertile imagination. No matter what the scale, extra personal care,

attention, and involvement in the design process can only benefit both the garden and the gardener.

When planning or renovating, a useful first step is to identify as many requirements as possible by making a garden wish-list of every necessary or favorite feature and function. As things progress, such a list can help confirm if your garden design is on the right track. This is an especially good idea if you choose to work with a landscape-design professional, as it clearly documents expectations, facilitates feedback, and encourages a solution that will truly address your needs and preferences.

The intention of this chapter is to inform and inspire the reader through examples of gardens seen with their houses. While the illustrations that follow do feature a diverse range, it was not always possible to include the house with every view.

To provide examples of period gardens has been a continuous but sometimes elusive goal. The illustrations in this chapter and throughout the book can inform us about the past in many ways better than words. If surviving period gardens are rare, many of their hardscape elements are still to be found. Existing period examples or elements have been assigned dates or other pertinent background information. Because gardens are lived-in and constantly evolving places, it is not surprising that the period design of many of the illustrated gardens are recently created interpretations.

Most of these gardens are the results of vision, hard work, and diligence: labors of love that evolved and grew along with the homeowner's skill, knowledge, wisdom, and patience. Showcasing the advantages of working with landscape-design professionals are the gardens in figures 34-40; figures 36 and 40 are landscape drawings including plant lists). Other such examples are referenced with names in the Credits section at the back of the book.

While Craftsman-style influences predominate, others that reflect bungalow diversity are included, such as Oriental (figs. 64-71), English Cottage or Tudor Revival (figs. 46-49), Swiss Chalet (50-51), and Mission and Spanish Colonial Revival styles (58-63). One should note that differences between these examples illustrate how some aspects of these designs transcend the particular style of a house.

29. Magazine illustration: "Every Garden Means a Home" (1916). This drawing appeared at the top of an editorial page in the October 1916 issue of *The Garden Magazine*, which was published by Doubleday, Page and Company in Garden City, New York. One of several popular American gardening periodicals, it was filled with articles on seasonal gardening ideas, and a few about home decorating and architectural trends. The house appears to be a bungalow with a broad shed-type dormer above its low roof that overhangs a wide front porch. On the right is a white-columned pergola behind a circular fountain, a greenhouse, and a small attached shed overlooking a tidy patch of corn and vegetable beds. At left, another utility shed is shaded by a huge old tree. Even if the family budget couldn't afford a lot this size, drawings like this one helped crystallize a popular image of bungalow living.

30. Overview of a model garden (1934). Illustrated in a catalog called *The Book of Lawn Furniture* published by the Long-Bell Lumber Company of Kansas City, Missouri, this garden illustration displays several components of the domestic American garden that were popular at the time. It was called "a striking example of what may be done with any piece of level lawn" with "no natural advantages." Its overall style favors the Colonial Revival, which had already been gaining public favor for over three decades. Some evidence of the Craftsman influence lingers in the random paving stones, the fieldstone foundation of the larger structure at the left, and the pergola beams. Spaces for outdoor living are important elements here, and plans for garden furnishings like the curved bench in the pergola at the right were also sold by this company. The strong cross-axial plan uses architectural focal points and a fountain to terminate views.

31. Front garden of the Charles Warren Brown house, Santa Monica, California (1908). This Craftsman bungalow is sited on a corner and has a minimum of gardening space between its front porch and the sidewalk. Around two sides of the house are plantings with low-growing habits, which create an effective buffer to the street. Their palette was kept in the range of soft lavender, purple, and white; deep purple *Intrigue* roses add a fragrant accent. Contributing additional texture and color to the garden are old-brick paths laid in a basketweave pattern. To vary their density and effect the brick-edged beds have differing widths. Accenting the dramatic upward turn of the so-called cat-slide roofline is a lush fringe of Easter lily vine *(Beaumontia grandiflora)*. (For other views see *Inside the Bungalow*, figs. 47, 96, 97, 99, 230.)

32. Front garden of a bungalow in Seattle, Washington (c.1920). Bursting out of its limited space, this corner garden spills out onto the sidewalk. Now mostly concealed by the recent growth, the slope of the front yard is buttressed by an original rock retaining wall that forms a small level yard area concealed in this view (see fig. 33). For this sunny location, plants were chosen for low maintenance, drought-tolerance, rapid growth, and plentiful color. Dominating the corner are the showy yellow-green bracts of cypress spurge *(Euphorbia cyparissias)* and the blue-violet flowers of the California lilac *(Ceanothus thrysiflorus)* that are set closer to the house. Other planting selections include broom *(cytisus albus)*, mock-orange *(Philadelphus lewisi)*, and lavender *(Lavandula officinalis)*.

33. Detail of the front garden of the Seattle bungalow. This private sitting area is raised above the street and hidden behind the dense vegetation. Leading from the front porch, irregular flagstones were used to create a pathway and a tiny bridge that crosses over a water garden to the bench on the terrace. The soothing sound of the small waterfall at the left of the bench provides a tranquil cover for street noise.

34. Front garden of a bungalow in Pasadena, California (1905). Recently created to complement a venerable bungalow landmark, this understated garden allows the house to remain its primary focal point. Most of its handsome Craftsman-style façade and detailing is seen in this view from the side driveway, which is close to the street. Low walls of river rock have been used because of their varied texture, for they handsomely define the perimeters of the garden beds and the driveway with their light color and rounded forms set against the greenery. Filling in some of the foreground at the lower right, baby's tears (Solierolia solierolii) seems to knit the river rocks together.

35. Fountain in the front garden of the Pasadena bungalow. Set close to the front door, this fountain provides a welcoming gesture. Bubbling water almost noiselessy spills over the rim of the urn and runs down its sides to disappear into a base of river rocks and plants. Simple, flat strips of concrete repeat the color of the granite river rock and outline the central lawn area; they also separate the lawn from a pathway of square stepping stones that runs parallel to the front of the house. (For other views see figs. 34, 36.)

36

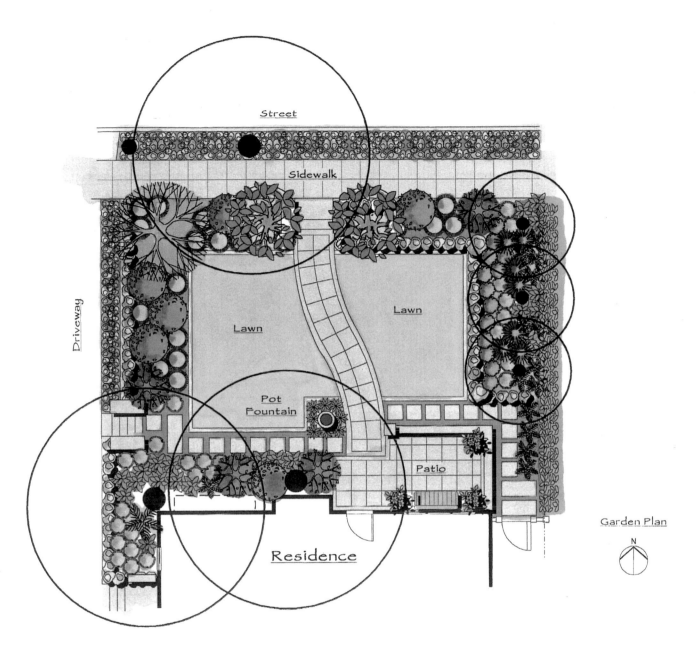

Street

Sidewalk

Driveway

Lawn

Lawn

Pot
Fountain

Patio

Residence

Garden Plan

N

36. Landscape plan for the Pasadena bungalow. Reflecting the architecture of the house, this plan is simple, but not without subtlety. The sequence of spaces that links the house to the street reflects the plan's composition of overlapping rectangles. Starting between the sidewalk and street, a narrow planting area expands the available gardening area. A wider planting area between the sidewalk and lawn creates a pleasing sense of enclosure. A pair of square columns frames the entrance, and their form repeats the end of the low stucco wall at the front patio. Inside the garden a wide pathway gently curves across the lawn, bisecting the slight downward slope toward the front door. The largest circular rings indicate the spans of the mature trees that were retained. This landscape scheme and drawing were created by Richard W. Fisher, A.S.L.A., of Toyon Design.

Plant list for the landscape plan in figure 36: (a) Major trees: camphor tree (*Cinnamomum camphora*), Victorian box (*Pittosporum undulatum*), fern pine (*Podocarpos gracilior*). **(b) Screening trees and shrubs:** hybrid madrone (*Arbutus* 'Marina'), camellia (*Camellia japonica*), lavender crepe myrtle (*Lagerstroernia* 'Muskogee'), tobira (*Pittosporum tobira*). **(c) Shady border plants:** spotted cast-iron plant (*Aspidistra* 'Milky Way'), Australian flax lily (*Dianella tasmanica*), creeping geranium (*Heuchera maxima*), Chinese loropetalum (*Loropetalum chinense*), lace fern (*Microlepia strigosa*), baby's tears (*Solierolia solierolii*). **(d) Sunny border plants:** golden yarrow (*Achillea* 'Moonshine'), pink gaura (*Gaura* 'Siskiyou Pink'), Goodwin Creek lavender (*Lavandula* 'Goodwin Creek'), Lindheimer muhly (*Muhlenbergia lindheimerii*), catmint (*Nepeta fassennii*), flowering oregano (*Origanum* 'Hopley's Purple'), upright rosemary (*Rosmarinus* 'Blue Spires'), creeping speedwell (*Veronica* 'Waterperry'). (For other views see figs. 34, 35; also *The Bungalow*, fig. 45.)

37. Dining area of a bungalow in Pasadena (1911). Occupying a deep and rectilinear lot, this area is situated close to the back door leading to the kitchen of the Craftsman-style house, and an oversize umbrella shading the table and chairs creates an outdoor dining room. In lieu of real stone for paving, random-size pieces of broken concrete were recycled from a driveway. Grass and other ground covering fills the cracks to hide the jagged edges, thus creating striking patterning. Clumps of wild grasses border the paving.

38. Vegetable garden of the Pasadena bungalow. Because they were considered utility areas, vegetable or kitchen gardens were generally placed out of sight of the flower gardens (see figs. 13, 16, 23). Given its own identity behind a low picket fence and a pergola-topped arbor, this example is allowed to interact visually with the rest of the garden. This photograph was taken before the major growing season was underway; a strawberry patch (Fragraria chiloensis) is visible in the foreground at the left, and a few herbs and vegetables are seen at the right, including the spiky-leafed artichoke (Cynara scolymus), a member of the thistle family. This view extends to a rear corner of the garden, where an arch-back bench marks a small sitting area.

39. Rear garden of the Pasadena bungalow. This view from the sitting area in a rear corner includes the enclosed vegetable garden at the left. Along the property line behind it, a high wall screens off an unsightly view and aligns with the garage and workshop building. To soften its lines, a shallow arbor that supports grapes and other vining plants has been constructed against it. Hanging in the center of the screening wall is a bench-swing from which one can survey the vegetable garden. Continuing the paving treatment of the outdoor dining area, concrete slabs form pathways that outline the flower beds and help to limit wear on the lawn during garden-maintenance activities. The tapering concrete pedestal at the right of the lawn chair dates from the early twentieth century.

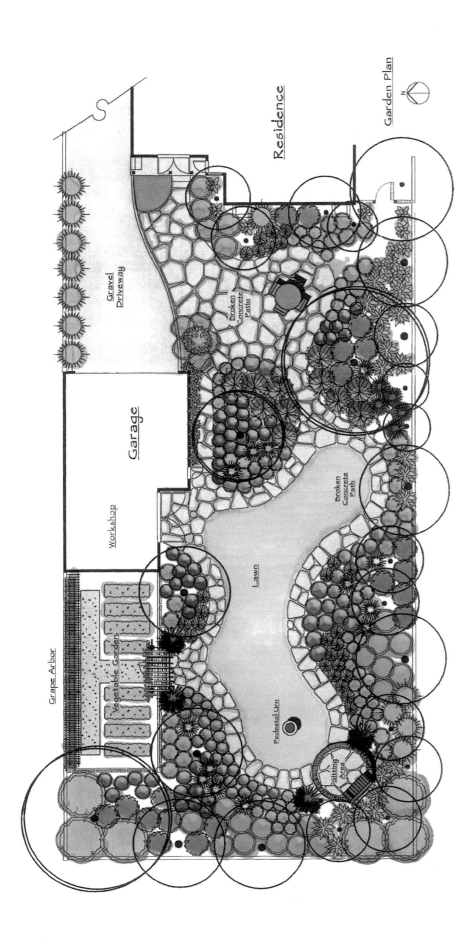

39

40. Landscape plan for the rear garden of the Pasadena bungalow. The decision to develop this garden using mostly curvilinear lines was determined by the deep, narrow length and rectangular shape of the available space. The resulting plan succeeds in foreshortening the length, emphasizing the feeling of width, and making the overall form of the garden far more interesting. A factor that was carefully considered was how different views unfold as one enters and moves through the garden. A rear corner was made into a sitting area; the circle of paving under it was raised a step and given a brick outline. A graphically strong element, the patterned pavement organizes and defines spaces throughout the garden. Beginning near the house, it flows out into connecting paths around the free-form lawn; the rounded dining area is emphasized by a large umbrella shading a table and chairs. Dining close to the house was a practical choice, and it also permits full-length views of the garden. The deepest and most densely planted areas were placed where they were most needed to create privacy. In a pleasing contrast to the curves, the vegetable garden continues the architectural lines of the garage and workshop. The circular outlines on the plan indicate the spans of the various trees. This landscape scheme and plan drawing were created by Richard W. Fisher, A.S.L.A., of Toyon Design. (See figs. 37, 38, 39.) **Plant list for the landscape plan in**

figure 40: (a) Major trees: Valencia orange (*Citrus sinensis* 'Valencia'), sweetshade (*Hymenosporum flavum*), fern pine (*Podocarpos gracilior*), purple leaf plum (*Prunus* 'Thundercloud'), pink trumpet tree (*Tabebula impetiginosa*). **(b) Accent or screening shrubs and trees:** angel's trumpet (*Brugmansia versicolor*), camellia (*Camellia japonica*), tangerine (*Citrus nobilis deliciosa*), lemon (*Citrus limonia*), grapefruit (*Citrus paradiso*), chinese magnolia (*Magnolia soulangeana*). **(c) Shady border plants:** Japanese anemone (*Anemone hybrida*), spotted cast-iron plant (*Aspidistra* 'Milky Way'), Australian flax lily (*Dianella tasmanica*), creeping geranium (*Geranium sanguineum*), hybrid lily turf (*Liriope* 'Majestic'), Chinese loropetalum (*Loropetalum chinense*), dwarf Oregon grape (*Mahonia aquifolium* 'Compacta'), lace fern (*Microleptia strigosa*). **(d) Sunny border plants:** hybrid yarrow (*Achillea* 'Summer Pastels'), Pacific rush (*Juncus* 'Quartz Creek'), Lily turf (*Liriope* 'Silvery Sunproof'), catmint (*Nepeta fassennii*), flowering oregano (*Origanum* 'Hopley's Purple'), pink penstemon (*Penstemon* 'Apple Blossom'), penstemon (*Penstemon* 'Midnight'), dwarf variegated flax (*Phormium* 'Cream Delight'), dwarf red flax (*Phormium* 'Dazzler'), May night sage (*Salvia* 'May Night'), fairy fan flower (*Scaevola* 'Mauve Clusters'). (For other views see figs. 37-39.)

42. Front garden steps of the Ellsworth Storey houses, Seattle, Washington (1909). Ellsworth Storey, a prominent architect in early twentieth-century Seattle, chose this site for his home and that of his parents. Sited in the Denny Blaine neighborhood near Lake Washington, the houses, which are attached by a glass-enclosed breezeway, are set in a large garden. This view shows the gabled roof of the original streetside garage behind a sparkling white rhododendron (see fig. 237). Surveyed by a white-marble eagle, a wallflower (Erysimum 'Bowles Mauve') provides a warm splash of color among the cool greens of native cedars. The tiny pinkish-white flowers beneath the wallflower are fleabane (Erigeron karvinskianus), which are useful for filling in blank spaces, but can also be invasively reseeding. The entry steps, built of local Denny Creek granite, are connected to low retaining walls. At the bottom of the steps on the right is a grinding stone (metate) from the Southwest that was used to pound corn kernels into flour.

43. Garden detail of the Ellsworth Storey houses. The houses were sited on a slight rise with views of Lake Washington across the downward slope of their rear gardens. Above the colorful hillside strewn with granite boulders, the windows of the shingled main house have the distinctive geometric divisions that were a signature detail of the architect. Convenient to the kitchen's covered doorway, a level outdoor living space enjoys views over the front garden. Nearby, a richly colored Japanese maple (Aceraceae palmatum) is used as an accent, and among the hardy plantings are at left yellow-green cypress spurge (Euphorbiaceae cyparissias), and wallflower (Erysimum 'Bowles Mauve') behind the large boulder; in the foreground are low-growing pink soapwort (Saponaria officinalis) and kinnikinnick (Arctostaphylos uva-ursi).

41. (Opposite) Front garden in Portland, Oregon (c.1915). An unusual corner lot, which was sited in the crux of a Y-shape intersection, gave this house a deep, tapering front yard, which has been developed into an asset by its current owners. In this view from the front porch a circular fountain is used to draw the eye as far as possible into the garden, thus creating the illusion of greater space. Also, there is a backdrop of mature evergreen trees that effectively screens out the street. This space has been made to feel larger by the prevailing use of curvilinear lines in its plan, which are seen in the rounded sweep of the brick walk and the free-form shapes of the planting beds that appear like floating islands in the smooth green lawn. Placed near the blooms of rhododendrons and azaleas, Adirondack chairs move easily to follow the best seasonal view. (For another view see fig. 114.)

44. Detail of a porch column of the Ellsworth Storey houses. Smooth river rocks cover this column of a portico sheltering the front door. An original feature, the bronze house numbers were pressed into a concrete panel set into the rocks and mortar. At the right is an Oregon grape (Mahonia aquifolium), and in the foreground is a native evergreen huckleberry (Gaylussacia brachycera).

45. Garden path of the Ellsworth Storey houses. Beneath the breezeway that attaches the two houses, a tunnel-like passageway provides access to both the back and front gardens. This path leads uphill into the front garden area. Along it, a naturalistic landscaping of rocks, ferns and native undergrowth give it the character of a woodland path. The white flowers at the far center are the early blooms of the Lenten rose *(Helleborus niger)*, sometimes also called the Christmas or winter rose. (For other views see figs. 42-44, 237.)

46. Garage with attached pergola in Pasadena, California (1913). Disguised with a home-like appearance, this unusual garage was embellished with a clipped-gable roof, an arch-top front door, and pairs of casement windows. The arch form repeats in the pergola across the building and again in the low brick wall, which contains a fountain with a glazed terra-cotta face that spouts water into a recessed pool. Most striking of all are the large outdoor-room enclosures created between the house and garage that invite many gardening possibilities as well as large-scale outdoor entertaining. Surrounding the rectangular lawn areas are rows of single columns and beams with pergola-style tops intended to showcase flowering vines. The architect was S. B. Marston.

47. The Ainsley house and front garden, Campbell, California (1925). In a remarkable state of preservation, this house was moved from its original nearby site to the civic center of the city of Campbell, where it is operated as a house museum. Now better known as Silicon Valley, this region was first driven by an agricultural economy that produced vast crops of apricots, plums, peaches, and cherries. The house was built for J.C. Ainsley, who had emigrated from England in 1884, and became successful in the fruit-canning business. He specialized in the export of canned fruit to England, where there was a strong market for California-grown varieties. The house was designed by architect A.M. Whiteside in the English Cottage style and its landscape was created by Emerson Knight (1882–1960) of San Francisco in the English cottage-garden style. (For another view see fig. 48.)

48. Garage seen from the pergola of the Ainsley house. Resembling many bungalows of the period, this large garage repeats the style and detailing of the main house. It once had living quarters for a chauffeur on its attic level, and today it contains the visitors' center for the Ainsley House. Viewed from a wisteria-covered pergola at the rear of the property, it is partly screened by a rose-covered fence. Re-creating the overall form of the original planting scheme, a lively border of mixed perennials and annuals curves out into a rounded corner bed of roses at the left. (For another view see fig. 47.)

49. Rear garden of a bungalow in Pasadena, California (1926). With rolled roof edges intended to resemble the thatching of an old English cottage, the house is complemented by this informal garden scheme that includes native plants with "water-wise" growth habits. A small wild "meadow" was the inspiration for the planting arrangement. Low-growing plants in the center contribute to a feeling of greater space, and include a variety of herbs such as thyme *(Thymus serpyllum)*, catmint *(Nepeta fassennii)*, chamomile *(Anthemis nobilis)*; the taller accents are clumps of native rush *(Juncus patens)*. Low edging plants include hybrid lily turf *(Liriope 'Majestic')* and native iris *(Iris douglasiana)* in bloom at the right. The best place for an outdoor living space was in a sheltered ell at the left created by a projecting study at the center. The space is paved with Bouquet Canyon stone, whose reflective silvery gray finish resembles water in the moonlight, and it is enclosed by heavenly bamboo *(Nandina domestica)*, crepe myrtle *(Lagerstroemia indica)*; and the fragrance of sweet or tea olive *(Osmanthus fragrans)*. The chipped-bark pathways can be widened or narrowed to allow for plant growth. Airborne visitors are invited to join an iron frog and floating camellias in the bird bath.

50. Bungalow near Seattle, Washington (c.1915). Perched on a sloping site and shaded by mature native firs, this house evokes the rustic charm of a Swiss chalet. Its modest proportions and dark wood exterior blend handsomely with the deep greens of its setting. A gently curving series of brick-and-wood steps and landings lined by lush clumps of native fern rise toward the house. The front door is reached across a deck that wraps around two sides of the house, and below the deck are masses of low-maintenance anchor plantings, including rhododendrons and native salal *(Gaultheria shallon)*. (For another view see fig. 51.)

51. "Woodshed" of the bungalow near Seattle. An enormous hemlock dwarfs this tiny retreat, which was originally built as a partly open woodshed. Located close to the house, it was remodeled by the present owners as a cozy den with many brightly painted casement windows to take advantage of the views and a wood stove to keep the chill at bay. Encircled by brick walks, a native fern garden thrives in the shady hillside location, which rises more sharply behind the building. A collection of vintage garden tools is casually displayed among assorted antlers and birdhouses on the exterior walls.

52. Front garden area of a log house near Seattle, Washington, (1910), and with a later addition (1994). A continuation of the woodland garden that surrounds this rustic house extends into this courtyard-like space between the original house on the right and an L-shape addition at the left. In this view the shape of the corner column of the front porch of the original log house seems to mirror a living tree at the left. The log construction and detailing of the original house was carefully repeated in the design of the addition. This project was awarded the Grand Prize in the National Trust for Historic Preservation's "Great American Home Awards" competition in 1994. (For another view see fig. 141; also *Inside the Bungalow*, figs. 16, 36.)

53. Front entry to the C. Hart Merriam house, San Francisco Bay Area, California (1904). Rough-cut blocks of metamorphous sedimentary rock, quarried in Arkansas, make a strong architectural statement in this sweeping flight of front steps that narrows gently as it ascends toward the front door. A generous front porch above the steps makes a splendid outdoor living room that spans the full width of the house. Existing plantings, such as the massive triple trunks of native California redwood *(Sequoia sempervirens)*, helped guide the final design of the steps. The sharp edges of the stone are quickly being softened by a variety of ferns, mosses, and other native undergrowth.

54. Porch and side deck of the C. Hart Merriam house. Beneath the sweeping roofline that extends to shelter the front porch at the left, a hammock invites relaxation. Blending the house with its setting, vines and window boxes perpetuate a Craftsman ideal that would have pleased Gustav Stickley. The house has seen very few changes through the years, and the current owners are committed to its preservation. The first floor opens directly onto this sprawling wooden deck, which provides generous seating by means of built-in benches that line most of the deck's perimeter. Three pairs of French doors provide maximum circulation to and from the deck. The house was built as a summer residence for C. Hart Merriam, a renowned anthropologist and naturalist, who was a founding member of The National Geographic Society and the Smithsonian Institution. The house's guest book reads like an early twentieth-century "Who's Who" of notable figures in the arts, sciences, and politics.

55. Hillside stairway of the C. Hart Merriam house. This fine rustic staircase relies entirely on the immediate site as the source for its materials. Its steps are made of colossal redwood blocks that were milled from old "high-cut" stumps on the property. Retrieved from elsewhere on the site, some decaying old redwood stumps were positioned in the grove to make it appear even older. Consistent with the oversize scale of the steps are the enormous stones that pave the area below them.

56. Outdoor room near the C. Hart Merriam house. The journey down the wooded hillside below the house on a steep trail of steps made from rough stone slabs rewards the hiker with an exalted version of an outdoor room. The cobblestone paving was salvaged from Victorian San Francisco. The built-in furnishings include massive stone benches, carefully positioned to appear as natural as possible. A stone basin at the left provides water for thirsty birds and forest animals. One of the multiple springs on the property supplies a steady stream of water ready for a cupped hand or container to catch it. The recessed fire pit is used by the owners to barbeque local oysters from nearby coastal waters, and it marks the heart of this area, much as a fireplace does for a home.

57. Postcard view of "A Mission Bungalow in California" (1912). Despite the absence of the rounded arches most commonly associated with the Mission Revival style, the boxy, low-slung horizontal lines of this house are relieved by the wide pergola that shelters an open-air living space. Between two shallow projecting rooms, the feeling of a courtyard space is implied without enclosure, and the front garden expands on this idea. A series of walkways form geometric planting beds punctuated by boxed topiary trees and carefully clipped hedges surrounding a central pool. This garden's formal organization recalls the traditions of Islamic gardens that sought to be earthly abstractions of paradise. This example must have been selected for a postcard because of its theatrical effect; so elaborate a design was more suitable for the gardens of more pretentious homes and was uncommon for just a small bungalow.

58. Hillside steps and rock garden of the Chick house, Oakland, California (1914). The garden surrounding this landmark house designed by Bernard Maybeck emphasizes the naturalistic character of its hillside site. Part stairway and part mountain path, this stony assemblage leads to a rear entrance of the property. Twisting through an impressive rock garden, it has a scattering of vividly blooming succulents that seasonally enliven the hillside's subdued palette. Influenced by Japanese traditions, rock gardening was frequently promoted in books and periodicals of the Arts and Crafts period as a way to recycle artistically otherwise unwanted rocks and stones. (For another view see fig. 197.)

59. Front garden of a house in Pasadena, California (c.1920). Not as common as the Mission or Spanish Colonial Revival styles, the Pueblo Revival was a style derived from the vernacular architecture of the American Southwest. All three styles had forms and detailing that recalled construction with sun-baked adobe bricks (usually rendered with painted stucco). In general, the landscaping of these styles reflected the dryness of the region, and so was particularly popular in the Southwest, although a few examples appeared in almost every region. The Pueblo Revival typically has squared-off rooflines and the appearance of thick walls that are sometimes "battered," meaning slightly sloping outward, as can be seen in the corner of the house at the center of this illustration. The use of projecting *vigas*, which are round structural timbers supporting the upper floors and roofs of traditional pueblo buildings, are also seen here. The dramatic arrangement of intersecting concrete borders emanating from low walls around the house organizes the garden into individual planting beds that spread out across the site.

60. Front garden of a bungalow in Altadena, California (c.1925). Resembling an early California version of the traditional English cottage garden, this front yard is the main garden for the bungalow, for it has the sunniest location on the lot. The most vivid color is found in the clumps of brilliant orange California poppies *(Eschscholtzia californica)* and golden-yellow sunflowers *(Helianthus)*. The gentle slope of the garden has been terraced into a series of raised beds, and their soil is held in place by movable boards. A network of surrounding pathways allows easy access for maintenance, and a small arbor for vines and some citrus trees are visible at the left.

61. "Before" view of the front garden of a duplex bungalow in Santa Monica, California (c.1925). This Spanish Colonial Revival duplex had potential: although small, its characteristic detailing, well-preserved interiors, and good location were obvious assets. But its street presence was far from inviting. After some building upgrades were made, it was time to consider the potential of the vacant front yard. Because of the mostly dry local climate, a drought-tolerant, low-maintenance garden made the best sense. A priority was to provide each unit with a separate place to sit outside. Another goal was to control the problem of rainwater runoff during winter downpours; it tended to pool up in the yard and flow toward the house, rather than toward the street.

62. "After" view of the Santa Monica duplex bungalow. In less than a year after it was completed, the front yard's new landscaping scheme has grown to a surprising maturity. Lined with small river rocks at the right, a new dry creek bed now cuts a curving swath between the house and sidewalk. A small patio area has been created in front of each entrance. Large enough to hold a few chairs, these patios were defined with slabs of Arizona sandstone. The creek bed was also designed to be a drainage ditch, so it was graded to change the movement of water away from the house and guide it toward street drainage. The creek bed also determined the location and selection of suitable plantings, positioned according to their tolerance for more or less water. Drought-hardy plants were used throughout the garden and a palette of reddish-bronze to burgundy was favored. At the center, red fountain grass *(Pennisetum setaceum)* is lit by the sun; at right are the spiky leaves of New Zealand flax *(Phormium tenax)*; and taller light-green shoots of white-flowering Matilija poppy *(Romneya coulteri)*, a California native. Beneath the windows at the left is the purplish-blue pride of Madeira *(Echium fastuosum)*. Other plants include reddish-brown *Euphorbia* 'chameleon,' red-blossoming kangaroo paws *(Anigozanthus flavidus)*, Korea lily *(Dietes vegeta)*, and Eulalia *(Miscanthus sinensis* 'purpurascens'). Bronze-red hopseed bush *(Dodonea viscosa* 'purpurea') is used for perimeter screening. Some of the low-growing succulents used here are *Sedum*: 'Brown Bean,' *Sedum* 'Spoonbill,' and a purple-blooming groundcover *(Productus purpurea)*.

63. Front hillside garden of a bungalow in Portland, Oregon (c.1925). Mostly comprised of two steep hillsides that surround the corner lot for this house in the Spanish Colonial Revival style, the gardening space has been put to remarkably good use. Enormous boulders hidden beneath plantings of rhododendron and juniper hold back the soil, and the showy beauty of this front hillside garden is best seen from the street.

64. View of a rear garden looking toward the house, Alameda, California. Being under the same attentive care for over thirty years, this garden brims with artistry. Many of its early plantings have totally changed, and its overall design has evolved organically rather than having been built to a plan. Although it is a highly personal interpretation of that aesthetic, the garden feels decidedly Japanese in inspiration. Lacking the solemnity of traditional Japanese gardens, this one was conceived as an informal place for relaxing and entertaining guests. Generous pathways paved with random stones sweep through much of its length, allowing easy circulation for large groups and simplified maintenance. Starting at the house, visible at the far end, several distinctive areas have been created throughout the deep lot. At the left is a sitting area at the back of the garage that is shaded by its extended roof. An open wooden structure supports a huge wisteria. Near the back of the lot is a large fish pond ringed by artistically grouped rocks and aquatic plants. A low wooden bridge crosses the pond and stepping stones lead to a tall clump of feathery papyrus (Cyperus papyrus).

65. Detail of the pond and sitting area in the Alameda garden. The open sitting area seen here, which is located across the pond and low wooden bridge, is also partially visible on the right side of figure 64. Next to the bridge, a stepping stone appears to float in the water, but is actually supported invisibly from below by a tapering concrete column that rises from the bottom of the pond, the depth of which ranges up to over two feet in some parts, so that unsuspecting fish are less likely to be scooped up by hungry raccoons. (For other views see figs. 64, 66, 176, 254, 256, 259).

(Overleaf) 66. Detail of the pond in the rear garden of the Alameda house. A closer look rewards the visitor with the garden's attention to detail. In a composition of elegant simplicity, four plain wooden boards are staggered to form the low bridge. Part of its structural support is an old post of weathered driftwood, which lends a vertical accent to the mostly horizontal lines of the area. A low Japanese iron lantern on the bridge lights the way at night. At the right are the pencil-thin stems of horsetail (Equisetum arvense) next to the solitary bloom of a Japanese iris (Iris kaempferi). The layers of flat stones at the right surround a small waterfall for the pond's recirculation. Behind it, the dog Klassje shares the owner's Dutch heritage. Her breed, Kdeshund, is especially popular in Holland.

67. Front garden of a bungalow in San Diego, California (1910). Peering out of its overgrown landscape, this house is reminiscent of some of the postcard views of similarly embowered bungalows that advertised California as the land of sunshine and flowers. A profusion of African daisies covering the foreground *(Arctotis stoechadiflora)* has merged with neighboring groundcover and shrubs in an effect that recalls a medieval *millefleurs* tapestry. Seen next to the spiky yucca leaves at the left are the blue flowers of a native California lilac *(Ceanothus thyrsiflorus),* a popular drought-tolerant choice. Tall spires of a cactus rise up near the house.

68. Rear courtyard garden of the San Diego bungalow. This tranquil, intimate courtyard greets visitors who pass through the side garden and rear gateway seen in figure 69. The courtyard's seamless harmony was greatly enhanced by a skillful duplication of the earlier building's architectural detailing. Suggesting an imaginary stream beneath it, a simple wooden bridge leads to the large painting studio added at the right. In addition to the vintage Craftsman-style lighting in this garden, the studio door was salvaged from elsewhere. The small gable at the center is the link between the roofline of the original house at the left and that of the new painting studio. It covers a small building containing living quarters, and its entrance is lit by the lantern at the left. The tiny garden includes Heavenly bamboo *(Nandina domestica)* at the left and next to the studio doorway, and an unusual fern-like potted palm of the ancient cycad family *(Cycadaceae).* (For other views see figs. 1, 67, 69; also *The Bungalow,* fig. 119.)

69. Side garden and gate of the San Diego bungalow. A completely different atmosphere is found in the side garden of this house, which was designed as a private, sheltered outdoor living space requiring little maintenance. An original river-rock chimney is at the left, and a whimsical cast-iron owl lantern from Japan lights the entry to the side garden. The simplicity of the gate and matching fence continue the Japanese influence. Stepping stones have been set into the paving except where they cross a planting area with a grouping of tall dragon trees *(Dracaena draco)*. A half-open double gate at the far end is framed by river-rock piers and columns.

70. Arbor and entry gate of the Keyes bungalow. In the modest spirit of a Craftsman bungalow, this discreet entry gate understates the remarkable property that lies beyond it. The gate is part of a fence of the same height and similar proportions that stretches across the front of the lot and effectively screens the house from the street. Just beyond the gate is a handsome arbor cloaked in wisteria and lit by a lantern. (For other views see figs. 71, 118, 119, 123, 125, 192, 199; also *The Bungalow*, figs. 36-41.)

(Overleaf) 71. Front garden, stream, and pond of the Keyes bungalow, Altadena, California (1911). The sprawling grounds of this handsome Craftsman-style house comprise only a remnant of its original lot. Listed on the National Register of Historic Places, this well-preserved house exhibits almost every desirable feature associated with the best of bungalow living. The impressive garden has been honed and crafted to its present state by its dedicated owners, whose improvements to the property are sympathetic to the integrity of its historic style. A meandering creekbed was recently created and strewn with granite river rock gathered from the arroyos of the nearby San Gabriel Mountains. The lushly planted lily pond includes at the right the round leaves of an Egyptian white lotus *(Nymphaea lotus)*.

Approaching the Garden
Entry Gates, Arbors, Portals, and Driveways

Like the front doors of houses, the entrances to gardens can make strong first impressions. They usually are more revealing about the space that lies beyond them, and thus can be even more welcoming than front doors. Surviving somewhat better than many other vintage garden elements, some completely intact or restored period examples are included here (figs. 76, 78, 85). Many useful period examples are also documented by the line drawings of figure 73.

This chapter presents multiple interpretations of "approaching" the garden. Most examples have closeable gates used with fences or walls and fulfill a basic need for accessible enclosure. The majority of these are not aimed at high security and tend to be designed as complements to the house as much as to the garden (figs. 74, 82, 84, 86). Whether locked or just latched, a gate draws the line between public and private space, and fulfills the common need for low-key deterrence of wayward visitors, usually neighborhood pets or children. Individual requirements will determine the influence that security concerns have on the entry's shape, height, and materials; a gate that offers high security doesn't have to look like it belongs to a prison, for it can also be harmonious and welcoming (figs. 81, 83, 87, 91).

If the primary entrance to a house is through its front garden, this presents a perfect opportunity to make a stronger design statement than might be required by a side or rear-yard approach. From the street, an entry gate can ensure a favorable first impression of a house. If possible, the path through a main entry gate shouldn't necessarily lead in a straight line to the front door, unless that is part of the intended effect (fig. 79). One way to approach the house is by a series of views that begin to reveal themselves upon entry (figs. 80, 88). Remember that a gate has the potential to supply mystery as well as privacy to a home and garden (fig. 85).

The need for gates at secondary approaches (such as to side yards) can also yield thoughtful solutions, especially when particularly visible or used by visitors. Some side and rear garden gates are often attached to the house, and their design should reflect that relationship (figs. 77, 89).

The gates for driveways (figs. 73, no. 14; 90, 92), must also be carefully considered because of their size. Some driveways are blessed with a porte cochère that functions as an entry portal for visitors arriving by automobile. These are typically integrated with the architecture of the house and are often visual extensions of its front porch.

Many house designs simply don't lend themselves to front gates, but give emphasis to the approach to their front doors through architectural devices such as arbors or pergolas. These can be used as framing devices that draw the house and garden closer together (figs. 76, 78), and perhaps also support some vegetation. Similar structures can be employed as portals or gateways between a variety of garden spaces (fig. 75). At times, aesthetics can rule over security: a particularly appealing example is a gate designed with an arbor that incorporates built-in seating (fig. 73, no. 9).

Homes Beautiful

CATALOG No. 28

Architectural Decorating Co.

F. J. HAHN, *Mgr.*

358-362 West Nickerson St.   Phone GArfield 1833

SEATTLE

72. Gateway design on the cover of *Homes Beautiful* catalog (c.1925). The Architectural Decorating Co. sold a variety of artistic ornaments for the garden, including benches and seats, fountains, sundials, birdbaths, urns, and pedestals, all made of cast concrete that the catalog described as "art stone." The designs offered were not as sophisticated as the design of this iron gate and flanking columns, which suggests the influence of Glasgow's Charles Rennie Mackintosh and the progressive designs of Germany and Austria (particularly those of the Vienna Secession) in the years just before World War I. Most of the pieces in the catalog were variations of the Classical Revival style and typical of middle-class Twenties taste. Although the cover design is unrelated, it remains a handsome example of progressive early twentieth-century design.

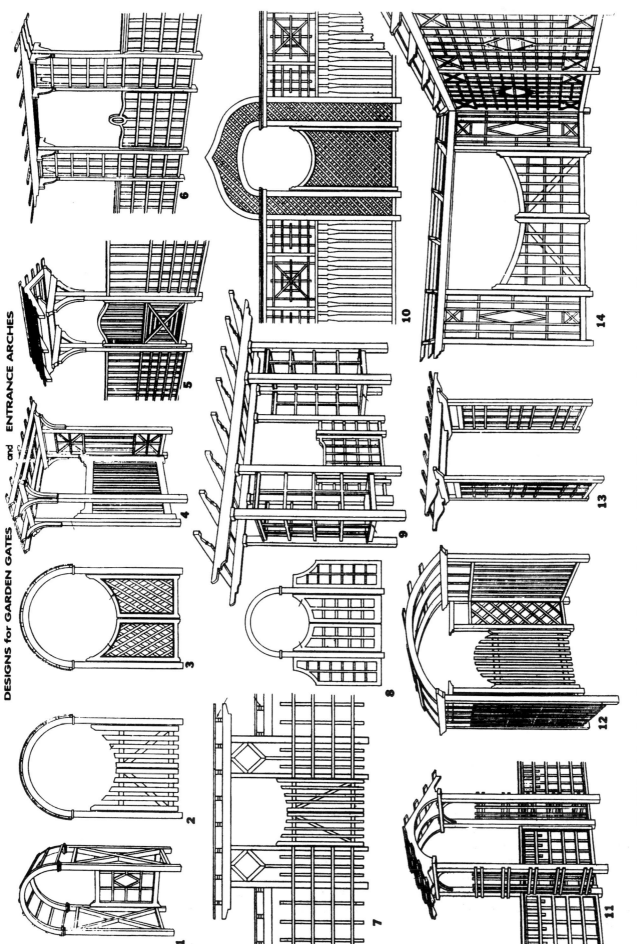

DESIGNS for GARDEN GATES and **ENTRANCE ARCHES**

73. Catalog designs for garden gates and entrance arches (1926). Published by the Southern Pine Association of New Orleans, these were designs offered in a catalog entitled *Beautifying the Home Grounds*. Most of them are very typical of popular taste in the previous decade, and show a combination of Craftsman, English, and Colonial Revival influences. The line drawings were intended as general construction guides with which these simple designs could be constructed from standard-size lumber. Although other colors were also used, they were most often painted white.

74. Front garden gate in Newton, Massachusetts. In a nod to the English Arts and Crafts work of C.F.A. Voysey, this design incorporates a heart-shaped cut-out in the center of its gently curving top rail, a device that often appeared on his furniture designs. The top of the gate echoes the arched entrance to the front porch in the background. (For other views see figs. 96, 234.)

75. Garden arch in Portland, Oregon. Instead of the more typical white popularized by the Colonial Revival, the color of this arch was selected to harmonize with the roses trained over it. The clematis beginning its ascent on the right side of the arch will eventually intertwine with the roses, and the arch effectively defines the garden from the lawn area. The form can be used in pairs or grouped in multiples to give structure to garden plans.

76. Front entry pergola and bungalow in Seattle, Washington (1914). Designed by noted Seattle architect Ellsworth Storey, this house was featured on the cover of the locally published *Bungalow Magazine* in 1916. A variation on the typical front-porch treatment, the unusual entry pergola parallels a projecting dining room on the right. A practical covering of tempered glass was installed on top of the formerly open-beamed pergola to shield the entry from rain. (For other views see *Inside the Bungalow*, figs. 85, 86, 117.)

77. Side garden gate with arbor in Marin County, California. Referring to the owner's ancestry—and for good luck—a cut-out in the shape of a shamrock pierces the top of the wide center splat of this gate, which is the centerpiece for an arbor made with two groups of four uprights that have flat caps. At the right is a red-leafed Japanese maple *(Acer palmatum)*, and a low-growing lemon tree *(Citrus limonia)* is at the left. Colorful borders of impatiens, members of the balsam family *(Balsaminaceae)*, outline brick walks with accents of handmade ceramic tiles.

78. Front entry portico of the Frank C. Hill house, Los Angeles, California (1911). Screen-like projections set on low clinker-brick plinths at either side of the front door support gently curved cross-beams to create an arbor-covered entrance. With notched and pointed ends, the cross-beams extend at each side in the manner of a Japanese *torii* gateway. Designed by the firm of Vawter and Walker, this house shows some influence of the work of Greene and Greene. (For other views see *Inside the Bungalow*, figs. 48, 49.)

79. Covered front entry and fence in Asheville, North Carolina. As with similar forms in Japanese architecture, a sense of arrival is implied by this gateway structure, and the absence of a gate lends a feeling of welcome. Striking a balance in its design are the delicate verticals of the fence and the suspended weight of the peaked roof. To admit light and views, the fence is more open near its top, while the tightly spaced uprights in its lower part create effective screening.

80. *(Opposite)* Garden gateway in the Windsor Square district, Los Angeles, California. With its grand ceremonial air, this impressive gateway evokes a sense of drama and anticipation. Substantial square brick columns with simple concrete caps support the weight of the heavy timber framing. The spreading form of the roof is echoed in a pair of hanging copper and art-glass lanterns suspended from projecting beams. This gateway leads to a large-scale garden in naturalistic style that incorporates native California plants; among its highlights is the skillful re-creation of a natural meadow garden (For other views see figs. 26, 27, 186, 245; also *The Bungalow*, figs. 169-172, and *Inside the Bungalow*, figs. 66, 219.)

81. Side garden gate and arbor in San Diego, California. A complement to the 1916 Craftsman-style house at the right, this side entry was designed to secure the side and rear garden without creating a forbidding effect. Capped by a red-flowering trumpet vine (Campsis radicans), the arbor's shallow peak has open-beam construction, and it is well-integrated with a matching fence. All were constructed of redwood and painted to match the house. At right is a pink-flowering Indian hawthorn (Raphiolepsis indica). Noted San Diego architect David Owen Dryden designed this and other homes in the North Park neighborhood and elsewhere in San Diego. (For another view see Inside the Bungalow, fig. 218.)

82. Garden gate and arbor in Berkeley, California. Framing a striking view that extends out to San Francisco Bay, this gate was designed to indicate privacy, yet also to invite passersby to have a peek. The gate's gable-shaped top with a slatted-screen infill combines with simple cut-out boards in the Swiss Chalet style and an asymmetrically curving top to give it a strong street presence. Beyond the gate steps pass by a terraced hillside garden and a wisteria-covered pergola shades a deck area fitted with built-in bench seating.

83. (Opposite) Rear garden gate in Portland, Oregon. This gate's simplicity blends seamlessly with the architecture of a Craftsman-style bungalow in the Irvington district of Portland. Both the gate and fence are of matching design, and their trelliswork supports climbing (Heirloom "Sombrieul") roses and remains open across the top for more light. Operating like barn doors (with pulleys on tracks), the two panels of the gate slide to either side, thus saving space. Built-in wooden planters flank the central path of irregular flagstones set in gravel. Pearl (a yellow Labrador) investigates the outside world through her own peep-hole that can be closed with a small hinged door. Pearl, who often stays in the backyard, is apparently less likely to bark at outside noises if she can see their source. (For other views see figs. 128, 139, 140, 170, 175, 239.)

84. Side garden gate and arbor with a fence in Pasadena, California. Faithfully re-created in this recent design are some original surviving details of the adjacent 1914 Craftsman-style house that was designed by Pasadena architect Charles W. Buchanan. Linked by cross-bars, the overscaled timbers used here as paired columns recall details of his robust architecture.

85. Courtyard gate of a bungalow in Pasadena, California (1911). Privacy and security are ensured by this unusual period gate that encloses the open end of a small courtyard. Created by the U-shape house plan, it allows inside rooms to have extra light and creates a sheltered outdoor room. Well integrated behind lattice overlays, textured glass is fitted into the backs of the gate and side panels to obscure the view without blocking light. (For another view see fig. 258; also *Inside the Bungalow*, figs. 53, 113.)

86. Rear garden gate and fence in Wellesley, Massachusetts. This rustic gate serves as a transition between the design of the garden close to the house and the wooded landscape adjoining the rear of the property. Fashioned entirely of small tree trunks peeled of their bark, both the gate and fence have three horizontals tenoned into thicker upright posts. Abutting open green space, the property is defined by this enclosure rather than confined by it. (For other views see figs. 232, 233, 262.)

87. Front entry gate in Pacific Beach, California. Part of a recent remodeling, this gateway leads to the entry courtyard of a seaside house. White stucco walls and wood create an evocative patina of age throughout the project that interprets the adobe vernacular dwellings of the Southwest and early California. The masterful execution of wood finishing for this gate and the ceiling beams exploits the material's potential for subtle color and weathered texture. (For other views see figs. 151, 177, 236.)

88. Front entry gate in Poway, California. The design of the wood-work, hardware, and masonry of this recently handcrafted gate was inspired by the work of Greene and Greene. It is the centerpiece of a larger ensemble that includes a roof covering with exposed structural timbers (partly seen above), supported by massive brick and stone piers. Beyond the gate a generous outdoor living space with covered sitting areas and a fish pond has the feeling of a courtyard garden. (For another view see fig. 265.)

89. Walled garden gate in Granada Hills, California. This recent adaptation of Arts and Crafts design is the result of a remodeling of a post-World War II ranch-style house. Walls of used brick are topped by the spreading open beams of a pergola roof structure, thus creating partial shade and support for flowering vines. Squared columns stand at the corners, which rise to form pedestals for low planters that are watered by a drip-irrigation system. (For other views see figs. 126, 150.)

90. Front entry and driveway gate in La Jolla, California. These entry elements for a beach bungalow have a clarity that suggests Japanese-design inspiration. Conceived as an architectural framework for the house, lengths of bamboo lashed to copper tubing form the screen-like fence and gate constructions, including those across the driveway at the left. Huge slabs of slate make a path of monumental stepping stones that disappear beneath the wooden flooring of the front porch. A spare use of plantings reflects the design's disciplined style. (For another view see fig. 196.)

91. Side garden gate in San Diego, California. Clearly inspired by the elegant designs of Charles Rennie Mackintosh's furniture, this wooden side gate of a Craftsman bungalow adds great style to a narrow space with little room for plants. (For other views see figs. 122, 241, 268.)

92. Driveway gate in South Pasadena, California. The only ornament of this new gate is the simple rhythm of its upright boards and its variation across the top of the gate. Inside the gate at the right, an area landscaped with rocks and a small water garden is illuminated at night and visible from the band of dining-room windows at the left. In the background, the double garage door has a similar linear pattern of applied moldings. (For another view see fig. 157.)

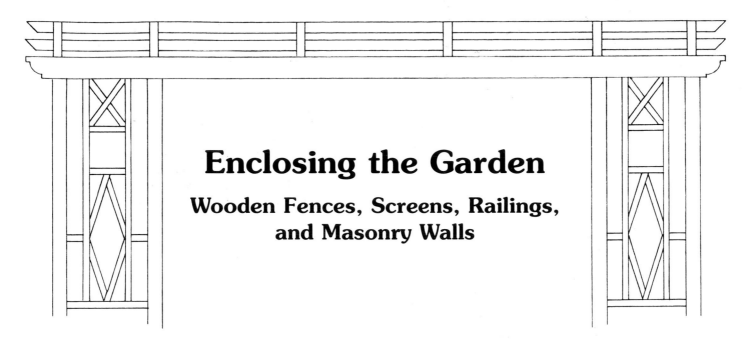

Enclosing the Garden

Wooden Fences, Screens, Railings, and Masonry Walls

Enclosing property behind a fence might be described as a socially acceptable form of isolationism; after all, it has been said that "good fences make good neighbors." With many houses surrounded by fences, many have mismatched styles. Today, few early twentieth-century bungalow neighborhoods lack fences, but most of what now exist are replacements. Fortunately, we were able to include several period fences and walls in this chapter (figs. 94, 99, 101, 104, 106, 107, 109, 110, 111, 112).

Because most bungalows were built on relatively small lots, the look of the surrounding fence was a major design decision (especially before the maturity of plantings). The most popular fence designs of the period (fig. 94) indicate that most people used to favor lower (or at least more open) fences than are typical today.

A compelling reason for the popularity of lightweight lattice fencing was that it achieved major design impact at very low cost. It used far less (and far flimsier) lumber than standard solid-plank fencing styles (fig.105). Lattice fencing was also well suited for the support of flowering vines (fig. 93), with which greater privacy could be quickly achieved. Although attractive, lattice lacked the durability and longevity of heavier fencing, and little of it survives from the period. Despite its shortcomings, it remains a viable choice for many of the same reasons that made it a period favorite.

For the naturalistic effects favored in many Arts and Crafts-influenced gardens, unpainted wood is generally preferred to white lattice (figs. 96, 97). The combination of white paint and traditional detailing (i.e. urn-shaped finials and classical columns) generally indicates the influence of the Colonial Revival style (figs. 93, 94, 95), the popularity of which became more long-lived than the Craftsman style.

Garden enclosures usually were most successful when they blended in with nature. An easy, inexpensive process was to build a wire fence and then cover it with dense hedging or vines. Rustic log fences were usually too labor-intensive (and therefore expensive) to construct in great length, but they could be used effectively for small-scale screening (fig. 98).

Few materials are as evocative of nature's strength as stone. River rock—the smooth, rounded pieces of granite retrieved from creekbeds—is synonymous with the Craftsman style. Most commonly used for house foundations and chimneys, it sometimes was used for retaining walls. When stone was used for a free-standing wall, it was necessary for stability to keep it fairly low (fig. 110). Because of labor and material cost, stone typically was used in small quantities and sometimes was supplemented with wood (figs. 106, 107, 108). Boulder-size rocks were far more durable for retaining walls than river rock (figs. 111, 112). Brick had limited use for garden walls because of cost (fig. 109).

Wood was the most popular of all fencing materials because it was easily available and easily constructed. The picket fence was a traditional favorite (fig. 99), for many variations were possible. Most wooden railing designs were usually Craftsman style (fig. 104), European of the early twentieth century (figs. 100, 101, 103), or Japanese-influenced (fig. 102).

93. Catalog illustration: "A Lattice-Enclosed Garden" (1934). Taken from *The Book of Lawn Furniture*, published by the Long-Bell Lumber Company of Kansas City, Missouri, this fence design has a top rail that dips and rises between sections. To allow nature to make the dominant design statement, the openness of the lattice grid allows for the easy interweaving of vines. The roof of a covered gazebo is visible beyond the open-slatted arbor cover of the garden gate at the center.

94. Garden fence and gazebo in Portland, Oregon (c.1925). Surviving better than most wooden garden elements, this original white-painted ensemble remains remarkably intact. The garden's general impression is a free interpretation of the Colonial Revival style. The mossy-roofed gazebo at the center shows an eclectic mixture of styles: its side railings are in the Swiss Chalet style, and its rafter tails and brackets appear to have a Craftsman influence. A round-topped gate (one of a pair) at the far end of the lawn flanks a section of diagonal lattice fencing accented by fanciful scrollwork. Centered on the rear property line, the gazebo anchors the axis between the back of the house and the garden.

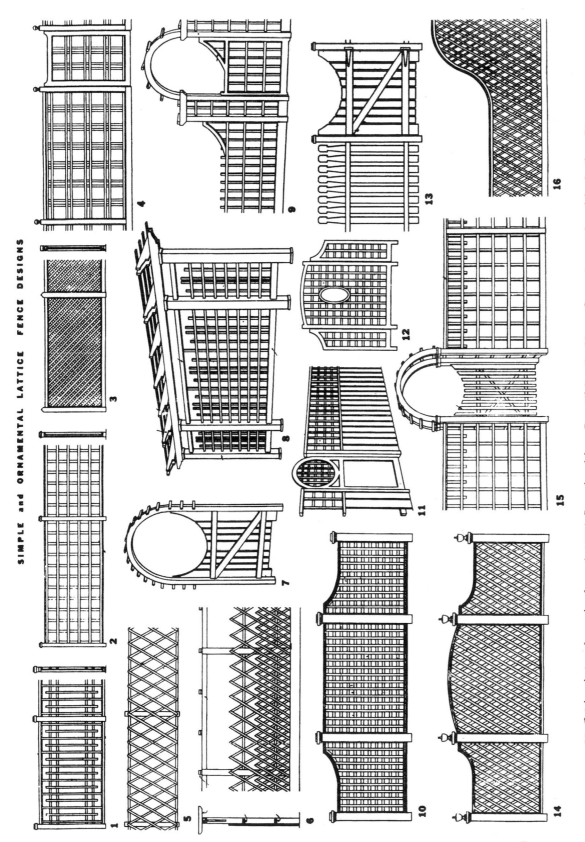

SIMPLE and ORNAMENTAL LATTICE FENCE DESIGNS

95. Catalog designs for garden fences (c.1926). Reproduced from *Beautifying the Home Grounds*, a catalog of the Southern Pine Association of New Orleans, Louisiana, these line drawings are suggestions for similar constructions that could be built using standard-size lumber. Most of the designs represent the prevailing Colonial Revival trend in popular taste, for the public's interest in Craftsman design was declining by the Twenties; its influence lingers in the pergola-topped examples.

73

96. Lattice fence and gate in Newton, Massachusetts. The sections of this unpainted open-gridded lattice fence are stepped to conform to the incline of a sloping driveway, and the tops of their supporting posts are capped with simple squared finials. The fence separates a bed of bountiful white iris in the front yard from the naturalized ferns along the drive. A curved-top gate leads to a front porch at the right. (For other views see figs. 74, 234.)

97. Lattice fence with twin arbors in southern Rhode Island. Architectural elements such as this one are used in a spacious garden to help organize large areas into more inviting arrangements of interconnected spaces. The area at the right has been carefully designed in contrast to the area at the left of the lattice wall. Serving as the doors between two large outdoor rooms, the arbors at either end serve to anchor the fence. (For other views see figs. 21, 22, 121, 137, 185.)

98. Rustic fence for vines at Sunnyside, Tarrytown, New York. This fence makes an artistic statement out of a prosaic function. Without its vines, it contributes handmade charm to the garden; when completely covered, it makes a fine decorative screen. In the tradition of the Adirondack style, it was crafted out of unpeeled tree branches that were selected for uniform diameter and interesting form. (For other views see figs. 3, 282, 283.)

99. Picket fence in the city of Seatac, Washington (c.1910). Designed in the Gothic Revival style, the staggered heights and varied scale of these pickets lend an unexpected vitality and rhythm to the fence. About five feet tall, this fence defines the property line that parallels a long entrance driveway. While the finish on this fence has an interesting patina, it is detrimental to the wood surface, and it would require major effort and expense to renew.

100. Railing detail of deck in Seattle, Washington. Enclosing a balcony of a 1909 house that was extensively remodeled by the current owners, this railing incorporates a spade-shaped motif with a long "tail" that recalls English and Scottish Arts and Crafts designs. The interplay of negative and positive spaces, always important in such designs, sets up a well-balanced and pleasing rhythm; the narrow verticals between the wide ones are the key to how well this example works. (For another view see fig. 263: also *Inside the Bungalow*, figs. 51, 72.)

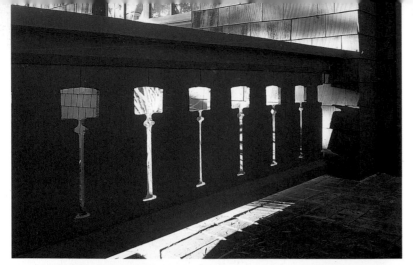

101. Railing detail of a front porch in San Diego, California (c.1911). This distinctive railing, part of the home's original design, welcomes visitors entering this gracious shingled house designed by Emmor Brooke Weaver in the Mission Hills neighborhood. Its cut-out motif was a particular favorite of Weaver's: a highly stylized rose whose subtly sinuous curves hint at the Art Nouveau style.

102. Garden-fence detail in San Diego, California. Inspiration from nature was a hallmark of Arts and Crafts design, and this fence appears to have been created to complement the verticality of the horsetail (Equisetum arvense) planted in front of it. The lightness of scale in its construction, given greater interest by the rhythm of alternating wood thicknesses, suggests a Japanese influence.

103. Garden-fence detail in Seattle, Washington. An exercise in pure geometry, this fence encloses the front yard of a modest Twenties bungalow in the Ravenna district. Inspired by the progressive early twentieth-century furniture of the Scottish architect/designer Charles Rennie Mackintosh, the fence is patterned with small repeating squares above narrow vertical channels of matching width. (For another view see fig. 148; also Inside the Bungalow, fig. 33.)

104. Railing detail of front porch in Berkeley, California (1911). Simple form, sturdy scale, natural wood, and the use of structure as ornament comprise the Arts and Crafts statement made by this redwood railing on a hillside Craftsman-style home designed by Williams and Winterburn of San Francisco. The protective copper cap on the post will extend the life of the wood.

105. Garden fence in South Pasadena, California. Offering a high degree of security and privacy, this robustly scaled fence is visually foreshortened and reduced in bulk by the planting insets along its length. Detailed with exposed structural bolts and simple metal straps, the fence was set in from the sidewalk to accommodate the profusion of *impatiens* that softens its lines.

106. Detail of a stone wall with a "window" opening in Point Loma (San Diego), California (c.1915). Unusual for a masonry wall, this period example incorporates along its length trapezoidal window-like openings, each of which is set with "panes" of wooden lattice. Designed by important San Diego architect Emmor Brooke Weaver, it once enclosed Rosecroft Begonia Gardens, a renowned nursery and garden that attracted visitors from all over the world. Founded by Alfred D. Robinson, it was a significant part of early twentieth-century San Diego's pioneering gardening community that included noted horticulturalist Kate Sessions.

107. High wall in San Diego, California (1904). This imposing, artistic assembly of river-rock cobbles and sturdy wood pickets originally surrounded Mission Cliff Gardens, a public amusement area overlooking Mission Valley, which once featured an ostrich farm. The stone columns serve as pedestals for unusual boulder finials that rest on their concrete caps. Overhung by the lacy, drooping foliage of vintage pepper trees *(Schinus molle)*, the wall is set back from the sidewalk to allow for a generous planting area in front.

108. Front fence of a bungalow in Pasadena, California. Here sections of wooden fencing have been set between concrete-capped riverrock piers on top of large boulders. Of simple board-and-batten assembly, the top of the fence has been shaped into a series of steps derived from the cloud-lift motif used by Greene and Greene. Part of a recent landscaping scheme by the current owners, the fence extends both the lines and materials of the 1910 Craftsman bungalow into its garden. (For another view see fig. 117).

109. Wall of a raised planting bed in Long Beach, California (1911). An original feature of an ocean-front Craftsman home, this wall contains a raised planting bed at the building's perimeter. The softly weathered red-brick cap on the dark, coarsely textured wall of clinker brick makes a striking combination of color and texture. These burned and melted brick-factory cast-offs became a building material favored for its color and textural irregularity by many Arts and Crafts architects. (For other views see figs. 116, 180.)

110. Garden wall with integral planter in Lake Oswego, Oregon (1929). One way that a stone wall can be blended into the landscape is by putting a planting recess on its top. As seen here, an attractive but otherwise inert element has been turned into a living part of the garden, resulting in a lower-maintenance version of a hedge. This house is a curious combination of influences: Arts and Crafts in the overall form of the house and the patchwork masonry of its first floor, Mediterranean in the red-tile roof, and Gothic in the pointed-arch windows of the projecting bay that forms a private chapel.

111. Retaining wall in Albany, California (1917). This pleasingly integrated effect is the result of a stone retaining wall that was set without mortar, which promotes the growth of small plants in its cracks and crevices. The cascading plant with the tiny blue flowers at the center is a semi-hardy, low-growing variety of rosemary *(Rosmarinus officinalis* 'Prostratus'), a good choice for hillside spots like this. (For another view see fig. 134; also *The Bungalow*, fig. 76.)

112. Retaining wall in Seattle, Washington (c.1920). Found in many of its neighborhoods, the massive boulders used for retaining walls may be the by-products of the extensive blasting and grading of Seattle's hills. These are massed into the sloping hillsides, leaving plenty of space for plantings. Sometimes referred to as a "rip-rap" wall, this well-planted example in the Ravenna district shows what delightful streetside variety is possible with wall-gardening. Here one can see lavender *(Lavandula officinalis)* at top right, and the shiny round leaves at the center are *Bergenia*, which has just finished its deep pink blooms. Small evergreens like juniper can also make good foundation plantings, mixed with self-seeding annuals like the orange-gold California poppies *(Eschscholzia californica)* at the left and the blue lobelia *(Lobelia erinus)* at the lower right.

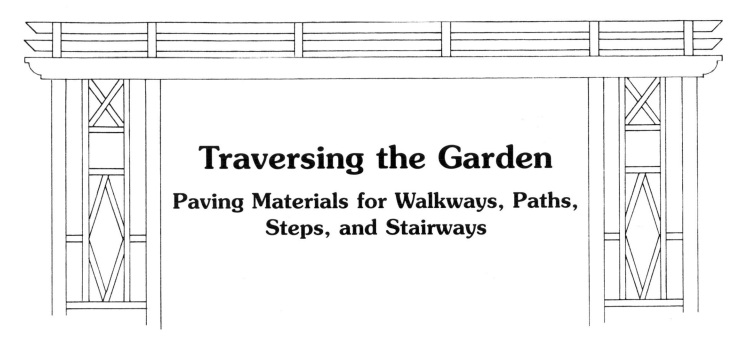

Traversing the Garden

Paving Materials for Walkways, Paths, Steps, and Stairways

Because most bungalows were built by budget-conscious developers, the walkways and steps in the garden were usually made of concrete to minimize expense and tended to be arranged in straight lines (figs. 113, 128). While original to many houses, concrete can be difficult to use effectively in an Arts and Crafts garden, and some gardeners have preferred to remove the concrete and replace it with something more in keeping with Craftsman style. A recycling of dismantled concrete paving that is gaining popularity today is to use the broken pieces as irregular paving stones and to allow vegetation to grow between the cracks (figs. 37, 39).

Next to concrete, brick was the most common paving material of the bungalow period. It could be laid in a variety of simple but handsome traditional patterns that gave a feeling of age (figs. 114, 115, 116, 117). Sometimes brick was mixed with other materials to make more personal statements that were usually determined by the mason (figs. 118, 119, 120). It also was popular for use in garden steps (figs. 125, 130).

Other irregular stones worked well for steps (fig. 134), sometimes with concrete (fig. 133). Flat stones, including slabs of flagstone, slate, or rough granite, were the most durable and serviceable choices that also offered many different potential applications (figs. 121, 122, 124) and are useful for steps (fig. 132). Today stone as a paving surface takes many forms. River rock embedded in concrete makes an interesting non-skid texture that can have an artistic quality when combined with other materials.

Wood was not often used for garden paths, but today railroad ties and other large timbers are commonly employed for steps (figs. 127, 132). Less effective where it is in contact with the earth, all but the most durable, creosoted or pressure-treated wood is prone to rapid degeneration.

To introduce vivid color on houses of a Spanish or Mediterranean influence, glazed and patterned ceramic tile was commonly used to face stair risers (fig. 129). Although ceramic and terra-cotta tile were among the most expensive materials for paving, they are extremely long-wearing materials and still make good choices for outdoor use today (fig. 126).

113. *(Opposite)* Entry walk to a bungalow in Pasadena, California (c.1910). Always a welcome reward for gardeners, much praise from both visitors and passersby is inspired by this vibrant display of Dutch iris bordering the front walk. Without a significant planting scheme to offset it, the light gray concrete walk would tend to dominate rather than interact with this front garden. Well anchored on its site, this home in Pasadena's Bungalow Heaven Landmark District commands much admiring attention.

114. Front garden path in Portland, Oregon. To make the linear geometric pattern work in a sinuous outline, the brickwork's basketweave motif required frequent adjustment to conform so gracefully. Running borders of single bricks laid end-to-end helped keep the edges uniform as the path progresses through handsome border plantings and ends in a series of concentric circles. (For another view see fig. 41.)

115. Entry walk in Portland, Oregon (c.1920). The herringbone pattern seen in this walk was favored by English Arts and Crafts architects such as Edwin Lutyens, who used its orderly effect to imply formality. Less common in our Arts and Crafts homes, paths of this type appeared most often with houses in the Tudor Revival style. (For another view see fig. 25.)

116. Entry walk in Long Beach, California (1911). Although unadorned by planting beds, this softly worn red brick walk makes a graceful statement as it approaches the front door. The "running-bond" pattern emphasizes the sweep of its curves, which are bordered by single bricks that are laid at 90 degrees to the walk. A unifying effect is achieved by the use of brick matching the path for the porch steps and column piers. Tastemakers of the Craftsman style recommended that an ideal front walk should express some of the beauty and interest found in nature, so a meandering line was to be preferred.

117. Entry walk in Pasadena, California. Large piers of river rock frame a curving pathway of irregular bricks leading to a 1910 Craftsman bungalow. The bricks were laid with a slight peak at the center, which sheds rainwater into side channels and drains it away from the house and garden areas. Recently installed as part of a redesigned front garden, this walk, ablaze with flowers, leads to the front porch from the side driveway. (For another view see fig. 108.)

118. Garden walk of the Keyes bungalow, Altadena, California. Sweeping around the right side of the front porch, this recently added walk of brick and random stone runs close to the property line, which is defined by a hedge of podocarpus *(Podocarpus elongata)*. Helping to add a feeling of greater width to this narrow area, the curving walk is bordered by a bed of river rock at the right and a crescent-shaped planting bed in front of the porch; the yellow flowers are Chinese lanterns *(Abutilon)*. The walk connects the front garden to a paved courtyard-like space, which has a raised sitting area in front of a family room that was recently built to match the original 1911 house at the left.

119. Paving detail of the garden walk at the Keyes bungalow. The color of the brick shifts from mostly red in the narrow walk to gray in this area, and the use of stone mixed with the brick becomes more animated. This view shows how the paved area widens considerably in the courtyard-like space in front of the new family room addition. (For other views see figs. 70, 71, 118, 123, 125, 192, 199; also *The Bungalow*, figs. 36-41.)

120. Garden walk in Los Angeles, California (1907). Wet weather made the paving pattern of this walkway more visible. Pieces of flagstone were randomly arranged with bricks in concrete. The pink lilies *(Amaryllis belladonna)* arching over the walk are called "naked ladies" because there are no leaves, which die before the flowering. A clump of feathery-topped papyrus *(Cyperus papyrus)* is at the right. (For other views see figs. 152, 153, 194.)

121. Entry walk and steps in southern Rhode Island (1930-1932). The decision to pave this front-entry walk and steps with irregular and closely fitted granite slabs has resulted in a seamless harmony of material and site. Mature landscaping and many years of weathering have tempered the granite and architecture, and the springtime display of a rhododendron in full bloom is highlighted against deep green foliage. (For other views see figs. 21, 22, 97, 137, 185).

122. Pavement at the rear garden of a bungalow in San Diego, California. A previously uninviting small rear yard has been transformed into an appealing outdoor living space by this paving treatment. Light-colored flagstone slabs are effectively set off by the vivid green of shade-loving baby-tears *(Soleirolia soleirolii)* in the spaces between them; this groundcover also blends the paving into the irregular planting beds in front of the house. Plantings at the left include red-orange clivia *(Clivia miniata)* and a Norfolk Island pine *(Araucaria excelsa)* rising above the garden. Delicate red-tinged foliage of heavenly bamboo *(Nandina domestica)* fills out the middle height of the planting bed at the right. The showy tropical leaves of elephant ear *(Colocasia antiquorum)* are seen against the fence at the rear. (For other views see figs. 91, 241, 268.)

123. Garden path at the Keyes bungalow, Altadena, California. Set into the earth so as to allow random plant growth between them, jagged pieces of slate pave this path that is bordered with bricks and leads to a sunny sitting area overlooking the front garden. Baby-tears *(Soleirolia soleirolii)* on either side soften the pointed lines of the slate. (For other views see figs. 70, 71, 118, 119, 125, 192, 199; also *The Bungalow*, figs. 36-41.)

124. Entry pavement of the Douglas Ellington house, Asheville, North Carolina (1930). Sited on a slope, this house has a shallow floorplan that is no more than two rooms deep, which avoided disruptive excavation of the natural setting. This narrow terrace area, created with random stones set into the lawn, is the primary outdoor living space. Although the setting is appealing, it is the building's unusual construction that captivates visitors. Difficult to label, its style shows a range of influences: some structural Arts and Crafts references are mixed with the detailing of a medieval English farmhouse, or some other vision of a storybook European cottage. It was designed by prominent local architect Douglas Ellington as his own home. He was able to salvage and recycle surplus building materials from his local civic projects, including yellow brick for the kitchen wing at the right from the foundation of City Hall, and the granite fireplace in the great room that was built with excess stone from a high-school project. Despite its relatively modern date, the handmade character of the house evinces a feeling of greater age. Starting constructon from a mid nineteenth-century log cabin, Ellington began to design and build the rest of his house in increments as he found inspiration, time, and materials. It remains in the same family today.

125. Step detail at the Keyes bungalow, Altadena, California. A built-in planting pocket of lamb's ears (Stachys byzantina) and a combination of paving materials give these curving steps sculptural interest. They are part of a raised brick sitting area that is next to a recently added familly room of this landmark 1911 home. (For other views see figs. 70, 71, 118, 119, 123, 192, 199; also The Bungalow, figs. 36-41.)

126. Garden steps in Granada Hills, California. Part of some Arts and Crafts-inspired improvements on a house of later vintage, these steps connect two levels of open lawn, and adjoin matching low retaining walls on either side. Pieces of slate, of a golden-orange color, pave the landing inset, and terra-cotta quarry tile, an almost indestructible flooring material, is used for the other horizontal surfaces. The retaining walls are faced with a rough mixture of brick and stone. (For other views see figs. 89, 150).

127. Front walk and covered entry of the Easton-Merz house (1910), relocated from La Jolla to near Poway, California, 1994–1997. It was Roger B. Mohling who had the foresight, location, and commitment to rescue this house from certain oblivion in La Jolla; he had it cut into three pieces, moved it inland to a tranquil mountain site near the city of Poway, and began its meticulous reassembly and restoration there. An important example of the modest but sophisticated wooden houses associated with San Diego architect Emmor Brooke Weaver, it is illustrated in *California 1910*, the catalog of the seminal 1974 Arts and Crafts exhibition held in Pasadena. Original features include the front door's fancifully curled wrought-iron strap hinges, and the handblown glass set into a grille of welded iron rings in the sidelight windows.

128. Front entry steps to bungalow in Portland, Oregon (1912). A recent renovation of this classic Craftsman home included major reconstruction of these generously wide front steps. A landscaped terrace at the landing level between the sidewalk and house includes a sculptural rock fountain at the left. The decorative cast-concrete effect of the large stone building blocks seen here also appears on the foundation areas and the chimney of this house. This treatment has been painstakingly recreated in this location to match the original work around the porch at the right.

129. Exterior entry staircase of Green Gates, Oakland, California (1903–1904, remodeled 1923). This hillside home was a brown-shingled Craftsman-style building and remained one for about twenty years, until its second owner remodeled it into a Mediterranean villa with Spanish Colonial Revival detailing. The height of fashion in the Twenties, this style often incorporates the vivid colors and patterns of glazed ceramic tile that is seen here on the stair risers that lead up to the main living level of the house. (For other views see figs. 130, 145, 146, 246.)

130. Brick entry steps at Green Gates. The idea of using plant material to integrate architecture with the landscape was a recurring theme in early twentieth-century bungalow garden books and periodicals. These brick steps seem almost upholstered by the dense growth of fleabane (Erigeron karvinskianus) that extends across the front of each riser and billows up on either side of the steps in a profusion of tiny pinkish-white blossoms. Shaped like miniature daisies, fleabane is mostly used for quickly filling in blank garden spaces, but it can develop into an invasive weed that needs to be kept in check. (For other views see figs. 129, 145, 146, 246.)

131. Entry stairs to a bungalow in Oakland, California (c.1910). Like many houses both old and new, the relationship of the front porch of the bungalow to the street previously consisted of a straight line that was a continuation of the old concrete steps at top right. The curving line devised for the new steps has transformed the house from the street, and in the process has created better distributed and more easily accessible planting areas. Buttressed with soil-securing boulders, the steps also function as a retaining wall; the color of their random flagstone paving is in harmony with the surrounding materials and plantings.

91

133. Entry steps to a bungalow in Oregon City, Oregon (1910). Requiring a good climb to reach its front porch from the street, this house sits high on a bluff overlooking the Willamette River, and rewards visitors with sweeping views. The route of the front path, finished in plain concrete, starts up a fairly gentle slope through a colorful, naturalistic garden (see fig. 24). Soon after it passes by an outcropping of basalt boulders at the left, takes a bend around them, and connects with a steep flight of steps leading to the front porch. Because the foundation and steps use the native stone as a building material, the house seems strongly rooted in the hillside. (For another view see fig. 24; also *Inside the Bungalow*, figs. 35, 225.)

132. Rear garden steps in Solana Beach, California. A graceful S-curve is formed by the sweep of this hillside stairway that is constructed with railroad ties set into the earth. Thus permitting a gradual descent, it winds through an impressively blooming stand of bird of paradise *(Strelitzia reginae)* that make excellent cut flowers. Taking advantage of this region's cooperative climate, the owners have created an arboretum-like environment of exceptional beauty, for this part of the garden includes many varieties of palms. (For other views see figs. 143, 181, 271.)

134. Entry steps to a bungalow in Albany, California (1917). This flight of steps was made of a heavily textured stone that encourages mosses and lichens to take hold in its recesses and creates a harmony with the landscape so that it seems "of the hill," rather than having been applied to it. Over many years, the entire hillside has evolved into a mature rock garden with a wide variety of small-scale evergreens, perennials, and succulents taking root along the steps in small terraced beds and along its front retaining wall.

Cooling the Garden

Water Elements such as Ponds, Fountains, Birdbaths, Swimming Pools, and Spas

There is a profound reason for the presence of water in the garden: as one of the Four Elements (along with Earth, Air, and Fire), water has always been revered as the indispensable nurturing force of all life. It has been used in the gardens of virtually every civilization. In the gardens of classical antiquity, water had a place of honor in and around the *atria* of many Roman villas. Surviving examples in the ruins of Pompeii and Herculaneum reveal some remarkably intact garden spaces where water appeared in gravity-driven fountains adorned by classical statuary of lead, bronze, or marble. Separate open-air courtyard spaces in the larger villas included an *atrium* (the space that was first entered) that led to a *peristyle* ringed by rooms set behind colonnades. A recessed pool (*impluvium*) at its center was designed to collect rainwater.

Water was also a strong link between architecture and nature in the geometric layout of Islamic gardens. A square area was typically subdivided into quadrants by water channels that represented the "Rivers of Paradise." At the center was a larger pool or even a pavilion. Many Islamic gardens were courtyard-enclosed, and their influence spread to Moorish Spain. The pinnacle of the importance of water in Hispano-Moorish garden design can still be seen at the Alhambra Palace in Granada.

Derived from Islamic precedent by way of Spain, fountains in bungalow courtyards and outdoor living spaces were influenced by the Spanish Colonial examples of early California (fig. 57). The use of colorful ceramic tiles derived from the same source (fig. 146). The Craftsman versions favored matte glazes and restrained pattern and color, exemplified by the work of Ernest Batchelder and others working in his style (figs. 147, 148).

The use of water in bungalow gardens derives from the importance of water in the gardens of Italian villas of the Renaissance period. These gardens served as highly fashionable models for early twentieth-century homes of the wealthy and were widely published and admired across the country. Water soon became another element featured in many modest gardens in the form of classically inspired fountains and birdbaths. Gardens with formal axial arrangements often had such elements to terminate garden views (fig. 145). Indeed, the renowned English garden designer, Gertrude Jekyll, described water as "the soul of the garden."

A very strong influence on the use of water in American Arts and Crafts landscape design was that of Japanese gardens (figs. 135-138), the effect of which could be found in gardens of all sizes across the country. If there was sufficient space, some kind of asymmetrical lily pool or fish pond was usually an important component. Along with water gardens that were typically graced with Japanese iris (*Iris kaempferi*), bamboo was also used to lend Oriental charm (fig. 157). Japanese garden style was prized as a solution for small areas, for tranquillity could be evoked by a rock fountain or a stone basin of water framed with a few artistically placed stones and minimal planting (figs. 139, 140, 141).

The Japanese influence was welcomed by proponents of Arts and Crafts design. Gustav Stickley featured examples of it in *The Craftsman* magazine, and it was widely covered in other periodicals and design-advice books. It was also to be found in public parks and arboretums.

Whether or not the climate permits use throughout the year, the presence of water in many American gardens has come to be dominated by swimming pools. Heated spas (also called hot tubs) are sometimes placed near the pools, but they are most often used singly in smaller spaces. While pools and spas were not part of period Arts and Crafts gardens, they can become handsome parts of gardens today (figs. 149-156).

135. Postcard view: "Japanese Garden of a California Home" (c.1910). This dubious assemblage of elements of a Japanese garden shows how misguided a Western attempt at such a garden can be. The garden utilizes a meandering, rock-lined stream as its primary organizing element, and at the rear center entry to the garden is through an adaptation of a *torii* gateway (such gateways are traditional for Shinto temples in Japan, not gardens). With a rustic-style railing that looks more Adirondack than Japanese, a thatch-roofed pavilion or pseudo tea-house overhangs a pond formed by a widening of the stream.

136. Footbridge over a pond in Lincoln, Nebraska. In the natural landscape of this region there is a preponderance of space, sky, and horizontal lines: a blank canvas on which to evolve a garden. Here a human-scale focus was needed to guide its ongoing planning; this large garden pond with a wooden footbridge was the result. It is ringed by low-growing juniper to keep predators away from the fish and dotted with floating water-hyacinths *(Eichhornia crassipes)* because of their foliage and delicate purple flowers. Strollers are led over the bridge through a patch of cattails *(Typha latifolia)* to a rustic seat of willow branches. Low maintenance planting selections that can spread and naturalize without constraint are ideal for such large spaces.

137. Garden pond in southern Rhode Island. Best enjoyed at close range, this pond serves less as a focal point than as an integral part of a greater composition. A pond can help create a greater feeling of intimacy in a large garden, also encouraged here by the lattice wall and arbor gateway at the left (see fig. 97), which imply separation from the area beyond. In a serene Japanesque arrangement, light and reflection animate this pond's dark surface, fed by a silent trickle down the face of the boulder at the right. A clump of umbrella plant *(Cyperus alternifolius)* in the pond and color variations in the surrounding small-scale evergreens offer visual coolness and variable texture against the encircling stones. The vivid purple iris spears, offset by accents of red-leafed plums, are counterpoints of color to this tranquil scene.

138. Garden pond of the Gray house in Los Angeles, California. Water can be an attraction for both eyes and ears in the garden. While this slender cascade aerates and recirculates, it also supplies plenty of soothing "white noise" that helps obscure urban noise, so that the movements of darting goldfish may be appreciated in peace. The pond's plumbing is concealed within the ivy around an old tree trunk. Glimpsed across the lawn are a raised terrace and other outdoor living areas of this 1909 Craftsman home designed by prominent Pasadena architect Alfred Heineman.

139. Rock fountain at the front steps of a bungalow in Portland, Oregon. A pleasant surprise on the way up the front steps, this sculptural fountain recalls Asian traditions of reverence for the beauty of rocks. The boulders were hand-selected by the owner according to a preconceived design. Set in a small circular pool where reflections amplify its size, the fountain recirculates water that gently washes down over its sides from an opening in the highest stone. (For other views see figs. 83, 128, 140, 170, 175, 239.)

140. Stone fountain in the rear garden of the Portland bungalow. Because of its low profile and placement amid plantings, this fountain doesn't assert itself. A closer look reveals a quiet movement of water emerging from a small stone basin and spilling into a surrounding bed of smooth gray stones. The small green object at the corner of the paving at lower right is a hose guard to protect the plants. (For other views see figs. 83, 128, 139, 170, 175, 239.)

141. Stone basin near Seattle, Washington. The weighty presence of this basin is tucked amid ferns and other shade-garden flora in a courtyard space formed by a recent addition to a 1910 log house. In this forested setting the basin is visited by woodland creatures in search of water. (For another view see fig. 52; also Inside the Bungalow, figs. 16, 36.)

142. "Wishing well" fountain in Monrovia, California (c.1925). An example of the overtly quaint aesthetic that was occasionally found in bungalow-garden furnishings, this fountain now holds only plants, but it still adds a cooling feeling to this shady spot. It imitates in cast concrete a stone base, thatched roof, and knotty logs as part of the Twenties popularity of fanciful English cottages. A throwback to Victorian taste, the cast-iron bench at the right symbolizes rusticity in its tangle of twisted metal branches. This area terminates a long leafy walkway, which is covered with an arching metal arbor structure that supports dense vines along its tunnel-like length, and they are part of the original landscaping scheme. (For another view see *Inside the Bungalow*, fig. 116.)

143. Birdbath in Solana Beach, California. The dull finish and irregular form of this two-piece birdbath of roughly cast concrete closely resembles natural stone. Its basin was too deep to be used by most small birds, but the problem was remedied by placing stones of varying sizes to form more inviting shallow landing and bathing spots. (For other views see figs. 132, 181, 271.)

145. Fountain with inset ceramic tiles at Green Gates, Oakland, California (1923). Shallow enough to function as a birdbath, this cast-concrete fountain was installed on the lower front level of a terraced hillside garden. Arts and Crafts influence can be seen in the small handmade ceramic tiles pressed into the rim of the lower basin. (For other views see figs. 129, 130, 146, 246.)

144. Glazed ceramic birdbath at the Alexis Jean Fournier house in East Aurora, New York (c.1910). Blending into its garden setting, this Arts and Crafts-style ceramic birdbath has a shallow bowl in consideration of small birds. Its base resembles a stylized tree trunk, the bark-like texture of which produced and created the mottled-green glaze over a cream-color ground. On land given to him by its founder Elbert Hubbard, prominent Roycroft painter Alexis Jean Fournier (1865–1948) built his home and garden bordering the famous Roycroft campus. Fournier created an elegant frieze for the lobby of the Roycroft Inn.

146. (Opposite) Ceramic-tile wall fountain with lily pool at Green Gates, Oakland, California (1923). Enhancing one of the narrow garden terraces that lead up to the house, this remarkable handpainted glazed-tile panel features a group of yellow iris portrayed against a sky-blue background. The tiles were produced by Malibu Potteries. Above the yellow iris a stylized ceramic dragon's head (probably Chinese) spouts water into a rectangular pool bursting with water lilies. In the water are more iris growing above the lilies. They are an aquatic member of the iris family (Iris pseudacorus), and their clear yellow flowers (now past their bloom) are remarkably similar to the painted ones. The iris is an ancient symbol stylized as the fleur de lis in the royal arms of France.

147. Batchelder-tile wall fountain and basin in Seattle, Washington (1922). Set on an outside wall between paired French doors, this vintage wall fountain makes a striking American Arts and Crafts design statement. The arched top, stepped form, and scrolled corbels are design devices often employed by Ernest Batchelder in his fountain designs. In this example tiles with a mottled and matte-glazed finish contrast with the low-relief pictorial designs of flowers and fanciful ships in the accent tiles. Tiny mosaic tiles in blues and greens suggest the cooling water that trickles down at the center. Living in Pasadena during the heyday of the Arts and Crafts Movement, Batchelder became famous for manufacturing ceramic tile designs, and he also taught and wrote extensively about design principles.

148. Ceramic-tile wall fountain in Seattle, Washington. Here is a masterful example of adaptive reuse, for this Arts and Crafts-style wall fountain was converted from a brick barbeque in the back garden of a Ravenna-district bungalow. Created from the former chimney at the left, the fountain is faced with skillfully reproduced Batchelder tiles that are arranged in a characteristic stepped design. The large tile panel depicting a pair of drinking peacocks has an opening from which recirculated water drips into a recessed pool, which was the former fire pit. From it a small waterfall flows into the rectangular pool which has a ledge wide enough to sit on. Next to a blooming lilac *(Syringa vulgaris)*, the wall at the right is faced with a tile panel with a motif of towering fir trees. The back wall supports a profusion of evergreen clematis *(Clematis armandii)*, whose clusters of fragrant waxy white flowers appear in early spring.

149. Detail of a swimming pool and spa at the Henry Weaver house, Santa Monica, California. This pool and attached spa at the center were discreetly fitted into the rear garden of a landmark 1911 Craftsman-style bungalow. The narrowness and plain finish of the concrete walks around the pool give emphasis to the planting beds along them. The handmade blue and green ceramic tiles in and around the pool and spa are an abstract reference to the Arts and Crafts character of the house. (For other views see figs. 173, 195, 247, 272; also *Inside the Bungalow*, figs. 32, 115.)

150. Spa with waterfall in Granada Hills, California. This spa area makes an Arts and Crafts inspired statement with its assemblage of boulders, brick, and terra-cotta tile, and it is the garden's major focal point. Grouped around a raised circular tiled platform, massive boulders help anchor the area into the hillside. The platform is reached by curving tiled steps that rise gracefully from the lawn and its uphill side is buttressed by low, tile-capped brick retaining walls. Supported on square brick piers, a pair of large copper lanterns dramatically frame the cascade of water over a brick wall, which then flows through a mass of boulders to fall into the circular pool below. The dynamic action of the water is also designed to be enjoyed in the spa, where the overhanging boulder forms have created a recessed grotto behind the waterfall. (For other views see figs. 89, 126.)

151. Spa and swimming pool with pergola in Pacific Beach (San Diego), California. Hand-hewn timbers of irregular form and length were used in the construction of this pergola that shades the spa area at one end of a swimming pool. The pergola's character is appropriate to the house, whose exposed wood detailing and stucco walls recall the Spanish Colonial adobe structures of early California. Its bold form and rough texture provide dramatic shadows on the soft red of the brick paving and the white stucco walls. (For other views see figs. 87, 177, 236.)

152. Swimming pool with spa in Los Angeles, California. An imposing river-rock retaining wall rises up to define one side of this hillside swimming pool, which was recently constructed to complement a 1907 Craftsman-style home farther up the hill. The use of river rock and random flagstone paving in the pool area are very much in the Craftsman aesthetic. At the far end of the pool, a short flight of stone steps leading to the house is nicely integrated into the adjoining retaining wall.

153. Detail of the Los Angeles spa and swimming pool. Built-in underwater bench seating at the perimeter of the spa and in the pool at the right creates a pleasant place to relax while enjoying the private, woodsy atmosphere. Arranged to appear as natural as possible, the loosely laid stonework that divides the pool and spa forms a small cascade of water that contributes soothing sound. (For other views see figs. 120, 152, 194.)

(Overleaf) 154. Raised lily pool (with spa and swimming pool beyond) in Santa Monica, California. The siting of a swimming pool and spa in this sunny rear garden of a 1907 Craftsman-style home was determined by the original lily pool seen in the foreground, which is overlooked by a glass-walled family room that was made by enclosing an outdoor terrace. Faced with river rock gathered from nearby Santa Monica Canyon, the lily pool's form, scale, and materials were the model for the new spa next to it. The bricks used as caps for the low walls and as paving between them were salvaged from the original chimney of the house, which was toppled by the 1994 Northridge earthquake. (For other views see *Inside the Bungalow*, figs. 228, 234.)

155. Recessed spa in the floor of the guest-house porch at the C. Hart Merriam house in Marin County, California (shown closed). The decision to incorporate a spa into an otherwise natural or rustic setting can cause design problems. A spa will have little negative impact on a garden design if it is somehow disguised, screened off, or otherwise blended into the surroundings. In this unusual but successful solution the spa is allowed to disappear completely beneath the decking. Thus the floorspace it occupies can be used for other activities.

156. Recessed spa in the floor of the guest-house porch at the C. Hart Merriam house (shown open). Like the lid of a large box, the wooden decking lifts up to reveal a bubbling spa ready for use. Its covered-porch location makes it appealing for use in all kinds of weather, and its outlooks into the towering trees of the hillside site are mesmerizing. (For other views see figs. 53-56, 155, 198; also *Inside the Bungalow*, figs. 29, 88, 104, 114.)

157. Illuminated bamboo and stone fountain in South Pasadena, California. Inspired by Japanese gardens, the sound of water trickling through a bamboo pipe into a stone basin at the rear center adds an element of serenity to this shady side garden. The area lacked sufficient sunlight for most gardening pursuits, so the owners elected to create a low-maintenance shade garden. Set into a bed of gravel and grouped around the water source, an artful arrangement of rocks and boulders makes the major design statement. Uplighting of a handmade clay mask at the left lends some mystery to the scene. A bird's nest fern *(Asplenium nidus)* at the rear right is one of the shade-loving plants used here. Bamboo fencing, assisted by clumps of living bamboo, helps screen unwanted views of the neighboring house. (For another view see fig. 92.)

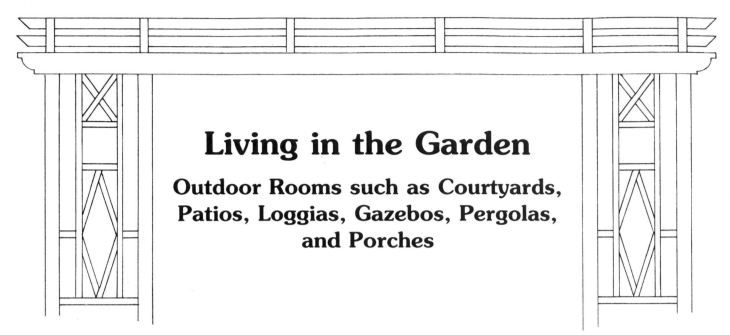

Living in the Garden

Outdoor Rooms such as Courtyards, Patios, Loggias, Gazebos, Pergolas, and Porches

An important facet of bungalow architecture was that it should be oriented to nature, and that its living spaces should be strongly connected to it. This was accomplished by means of many windows and French doors to provide plenty of air and views, and sometimes extra outside doors leading to both primary and secondary living spaces. Because of the prominence of front porches and the popularity of sleeping porches, most bungalows clearly show the belief that fresh air was essential for good health.

Because the front porch usually adjoined the living room, it was the most commonly utilized of all outdoor living spaces (figs. 168, 169, 171, 172, 173). Integral with the architecture of the house, it was the primary transition space between exterior and interior, and it was frequently described by Gustav Stickley and other period tastemakers as the "outdoor living room." Although less common, some homes featured outdoor living spaces on other sides of the house (figs. 163, 168, 174). They appeared sometimes with open-beamed pergola-style roofs (figs. 161, 166) or entirely open-air deck spaces (fig. 160).

Although most were first constructed as outdoor rooms, many porches of homes in colder or wetter climates were later glass-enclosed so as to be usable without much concern for the weather (fig. 174). Some of these spaces had glass enclosures like storm windows that were removable and then replaced in the warmer months with screens, which better preserved their outdoor character. With space at a premium in many bungalows, many porches have been turned into strictly interior spaces.

Few plans were better at merging indoor and outdoor living than those with rooms arranged around a central open courtyard space, which allowed interaction between house and garden from almost every room in the house (figs. 158, 159). While courtyard plans tended to be most practical in milder climates, examples appeared across the country. In colder locations the courtyard was sometimes glass-covered.

Moving further into the garden, a wide variety of outdoor living spaces was possible. Depending on the space available, some were simply extensions of those attached to the house (fig. 162). Others could be entirely independent but complementary architectural entities in the form of a covered garden pavilion (figs. 164, 175) or gazebo, sometimes also referred to as a summerhouse. A popular accent structure for bungalow gardens was the free-standing open-beamed pergola that could also display flowering vines. Taking many forms, it often sheltered paved seating areas (figs. 165, 167). Other open-air spaces could be defined only by paving or possibly as a raised deck without a covering (fig. 176).

To remedy a common condition, some of the most successful examples of recent bungalow remodels are those that improve interior access to the garden from the rear-facing rooms (fig. 179). The bungalow's most garden-friendly outside space, the porch, was generally on the front of the house and interacted with the living room that was usually located there. Although many kitchens faced toward the back, their rear door was usually considered to be a utility entrance, and it often included a service porch. This is one of the most popular places to consider remodeling in order to make a larger kitchen and have better access to the garden. Since at least one bedroom also typically faces toward the back, it is less likely originally to have had an outside door. In lieu of an original master bedroom, many such bungalow bedrooms are being extended further and opened into their gardens.

Other recent remodels have created entirely new outdoor rooms with luxurious proportions, striking architectural character, and period inspiration. An effective way to expand living space on the front of an otherwise bland, disfigured, or later-period house is by enclosing its available street-side space with high walls to create an entry with a private courtyard feeling (fig. 181). Directly adjoining the front door, such spaces can expand outdoor living space in a very convenient location. Features such as working fireplaces and pergola-style roof beams can further reinforce a room-like atmosphere (figs. 180, 181). Some imaginative contemporary examples have interpreted the bungalow tradition of indoor-outdoor living in a more abstract way (fig. 178), showing a promising direction for new construction that appears inspired by the Craftsman style.

158. View of a bungalow courtyard illustrated in *The Craftsman* magazine, July 1904. Since ancient times, houses with courtyards have provided some of the best examples of well-integrated indoor-outdoor living spaces: quintessential outdoor rooms that harmoniously combine the built and natural environments. Gustav Stickley admired the use of courtyards he had seen in California, and was inspired by the architecture of old adobe Missions and haciendas. This appealing view would have been seen from the living and dining rooms along the front side of the house. In addition, kitchen and utility space would have been to the right, and bedrooms to the left. The small lily pool with a fountain of boulders was recommended as a focal point, and surrounding veranda areas, protected by roof overhangs, were to be furnished as outdoor living rooms. The veranda spaces were used as the primary circulation between rooms, and the columns could be softened by climbing vines.

159. Courtyard bungalow in Portland, Oregon (1908). A pergola with mature grapevines partially encloses the open end of this bungalow's outdoor courtyard. Oriented toward a private side garden rather than a distant view, the courtyard of this Irvington-district house features a large raised fountain with a statue at its center, which is surrounded by two tiers of planter boxes for seasonal gardening. A remodeled kitchen now opens to the courtyard's inner side, while bedrooms occupy the left wing, and the living room (with the dining room, beyond it) is through the French doors at the right. Sheltering another outdoor sitting area at the right, the pergola visually extends the house into the garden. (This house makes an interesting comparison to a view of the larger Lanterman house illustrated in *The Bungalow,* fig. 128).

160. Postcard view: "Living Room in a Live Oak" (1908). Childhood fantasies of treetop living are here given the grown-up twist of adult furnishings and suspended electric lighting. In this unusual period example the "treehouse" was probably a deck attached to a hillside house and was constructed to accommodate existing trees. The location was probably somewhere in California where year-round outdoor living was often illustrated on postcards. Considered by period tastemakers as appropriate handmade accessories for Arts and Crafts rooms, geometric-patterned rugs in the Native American style are shown here with chairs of simple lines, for such furnishings were recommended for the well-outfitted front porch of a bungalow. Cradled in the arms of nature in an era without radio and television, a likely purpose for this retreat is suggested by the table of reading material and the light above it.

Living Room in a Live Oak.

161. *(Opposite)* Detail of the pergola at El Retiro, the Lanterman house, La Cañada-Flintridge, California (1915). An airy canopy of wisteria covers the handsome pergola of this oversized Craftsman-style bungalow, whose extraordinary period interiors are open to the public as a house museum. This pergola encloses three sides of the sprawling home, including the open end of a three-sided courtyard. The meticulous restoration of the exterior included exact duplication of the original concrete columns.

162. Front patio of a bungalow in Santa Monica, California (c.1900). Wrapping around the small house in an L-shape, this patio area continues into a side garden at the right. In a climate that makes outdoor living possible all year, this expanse of open space allows the small house to appear larger, a feeling that is enhanced by the level of the brick paving being close to that of the adjoining interior spaces. The use of many container plants allows for flexible rearrangement according to seasonal and maintenance needs.

163. Outdoor seating area of a loggia in Los Angeles, California (1910). One of the best of all outdoor-room arrangements, a loggia allows the cozy feeling of enclosure that a courtyard provides with the added bonus of a sheltering roof. The deeply cushioned bamboo furniture shown here provides living-room luxury. An original part of a Craftsman-style home designed by Sumner Hunt, this loggia has retained its thick terra-cotta paving tile. It faces a sunny open patio, and directly opposite is a wall fountain and lily pool. The loggia's scale is similar to a generous front porch, but with more privacy and without the usual columns. Its deep overhang keeps the region's strong light under control, and the French doors allow easy access to the rest of the house. (For another view see fig. 191.)

164. Viewing pavilion in Asheville, North Carolina (c.1925). Sited on public land, this charming little building offers a spot to rest while hiking up or down a wooded hillside. Seen here on a moody day in late winter, it helps to remind us that nature offers beauty at any time of the year, and temporarily leafless trees permit distant views from this steep perch. Its rustic construction, similar to some of the architecture of public buildings in our National Parks, has oversize columns of local stone that support an overhanging peaked roof with exposed timber framing. The stones in the foreground outline a walking trail, hidden by fallen leaves, that passes through the structure as it continues on its way into the woods.

165. Postcard view: "Poinsettia Hedge in Blossom—Winter Scene in California" (1912). Overlooked by a Craftsman-style bungalow at the right, the focus of this garden appears to be on an oversize outdoor living area shaded by the unpainted crossing beams of a pergola that contrast with the pristine white of the classical columns. An extravagant display of poinsettias creates a tall privacy screen for the pergola. This postcard exemplifies the common notion that California was a land of plenty, where anything could happen, and where almost anything would *grow*.

166. Pergola attached to a bungalow in Piedmont, California (1919). The usable space of a bungalow's living room was expanded by this simple lattice-framed pergola, which was built around the French doors at the right. Few examples survive from the period because their lightweight wood construction was prone to deterioration. Enormously popular across America, such inexpensive wooden structures were sometimes built by handy homeowners from the simple plans that were readily available from lumber companies. (For another view see fig. 238; also *Inside the Bungalow*, figs. 134-137.)

167. Viewing pergola in Balboa Park, San Diego, California (c.1922). This period structure is rare, and it shows how a simple wooden design can still have an informal elegance. It has probably survived because of the massive scale of the timbers. Cloaked in its original trumpet vine *(Campsis radicans)*, it was designed as a viewing promenade along the top of a small ravine, but its outlook is now somewhat reduced by the park's mature trees.

168. Side porch of a bungalow in Long Beach, California (1913). Located in the Rose Park Historical district, this narrow side porch is adjoined by the dining room through French doors at the right and a separate breakfast room through a door at the far end. Although its compact size doesn't allow much furniture, it is obvious that Magic, the resident cat, is completely happy in the first bamboo-framed lounge chair. A bougainvillea *(Bougainvillea spectabilis)* hangs from the eaves. A tall hedge creates good privacy at the property line, and a typical small detached garage is at the back of the lot. The driveway's central plot, usually given over to lawn between two strips of concrete, is also typical of many bungalows, and it relieves the severity of too much concrete or asphalt. It is another bungalow idea that is worthy of consideration today. (For other views see *Inside the Bungalow*, figs. 15, 67.)

169. *(Opposite)* Wisteria-covered pergola porch in San Diego, California (1906). A classic component of Arts and Crafts gardens everywhere, a venerable wisteria vine drapes the clinker-brick column, and gorgeously entwines the open beams of the pergola above. The brick continues around the porch as a low wall, creating greater privacy for the original slat-back porch swing behind it. Consistent with the style portrayed in many period images of bungalow gardens are the informality and somewhat overgrown quality of these plantings. (For other views see *Inside the Bungalow*, figs. 63, 179, 210.)

170. Detail of a bungalow front porch in Portland, Oregon (1912). The front porch, the bungalow's window on the world, is often the most important outdoor living space, for it permits easy communication with neighbors who pass by, thus helping to create a greater feeling of community. The recent major effort to restore this bungalow included an overhaul of its front steps and roomy front porch; the cast-concrete that imitates stone blocks in the columns is original to the house. Adding soft illumination after dark, unobtrusive uplighting is tucked on top of the column at the corner. The large pot at the right of the swing is adapted from an original design by Gertrude Jekyll, the important English gardening expert of the Arts and Crafts period. (For other views see figs. 83, 128, 139, 140, 175, 239.)

171. Pergola porch in South Pasadena, California (c.1907). An inviting area of partial shade and period atmosphere, the design of this front porch admits light into the front rooms of the house through the open-beamed pergola roof. Supported on hefty columns of clinker brick and river rock, the pergola allows flowering vines to soften its timbers. The masonry style is similar to that used by Greene and Greene, and its combination of smooth and rough textures earned it the catchy nickname of "the Peanut-Brittle style." The concrete paving surface of the porch is scored to resemble large tiles. (For other views see figs. 189, 193, 243.)

172. Front porch in Pasadena, California (c.1910). This shingled Craftsman-style house was recently painted in rich shades of green and rust. Container plants grouped on and around the porch and steps help to blend them into the garden. A planting bed along the porch foundation, created by a low rock retaining wall, contains a vintage ceramic birdbath. Informality and extra light to the interior are provided by identical pairs of French doors that lead to the main entry and living room.

173. Front porch of the Henry Weaver house, Santa Monica, California (1911). Equipped as a luxurious outdoor living room, this porch justifies its decor by offering splendid views extending to the ocean. The porch columns are set in groups and linked by substantial tenons; the pale limestone-colored brick of their piers continues in a low railing wall. Corbeling above the columns, which repeats in the projecting beams of the roof, creates stepped frames for the views. These columns make an interesting comparison to those in figure 171. After sustaining major damage in the 1994 Northridge earthquake, the house has been skillfully restored to its original condition. (For other views see figs. 149, 195, 247, 272.)

174. Sun porch at Sconehenge in Plymouth, Massachusetts (1910). Once open to the elements, this porch remains a sun-warmed and light-filled space that connects the living room at the left to a recently restored deck area across the back of this Colonial Revival house. Retained after its enclosure in the Twenties are shingled walls and a wood tongue-and-groove ceiling. Now operated as a bed and breakfast inn, the atmospheric house is full of fascinating collectibles and curiosities like the woodland creatures seen here. (For another view see fig. 190.)

175. Garden pavilion and potting shed of a bungalow in Portland, Oregon. Rather than reconstruct a detached back-corner garage, the current owners replaced it with a structure that fulfilled their specific needs. Architecturally sympathetic to the house, the new structure repeats some of its Craftsman detailing and covers the same area of the old garage, but it is now a shelter for people to sit and enjoy the garden. Concealed behind the doors at the back is a roomy potting shed with storage for garden tools as well as counter space that is convenient for outdoor entertaining. Irregular brick paving extends into this area from the former driveway and continues at the right into an open patio area next to the house. The planting pocket with pebbles and grasses at the base of the column at the right contains the fountain in a small stone basin shown in figure 140.

176. Raised sitting area with an aviary in Alameda, California. A slight change of level, rather than an enclosure or overhead construction, sets this area apart. At the left, a small yet complex pergola displays a vine and forms a subtle barrier on one side. At the right, an aviary set on a river-rock foundation houses a family of cheerful finches. A collection of favorite container plants makes this a handsome place to work or rest.

177. Veranda in Pacific Beach (San Diego), California. Interpreting the Spanish Colonial adobe architecture of early California, a shady and atmospheric veranda wraps around this house. The simple framing of this roof remains exposed; one can see the undersides of its terra-cotta roof tiles. The continuous overhang completely shadows the walls, thus providing a cool place to sit or stroll. Low-maintenance gardening close to the house consists of trailing vines framing the views and groups of potted plants. (For other views see figs. 87, 151, 236.)

178. *(Opposite)* Outdoor living area of a beach house in Leucadia, California. This sleek contemporary house deserves appreciation for its creative abstraction of Craftsman forms. Entered through a door of modern art-glass panels, this court-yard-like space permits covered passage to the interior of the house through doors ahead and at the right, and the ocean is visible through one of them. Overhead, recalling the shed-roof forms of Craftsman-style porches, a sloping glass roof is set into a simple framework of sandblasted wooden timbers. Square tapering columns are made of concrete. Their surfaces retain the imprint of their wooden forms, and they are accented on one side by narrow handmade tiles. Set amid drought-tolerant plantings, the built-in outdoor "furniture" at the left is also cast concrete. Inside the house immense sliding-glass panels can be opened to the ocean view.

179. Pergola-covered rear terrace of a bungalow in Pasadena, California. Recently added to the rear of this bungalow to improve access to the garden and expand out-door living space, this handsome attached pergola repeats original design details from the front of the house in its columns and beam ends. The floor level of the terrace, although up three steps from the garden level, does not reach the height of the door sills so as to ensure the complete runoff of water. A fine-mesh nylon screen has been attached across the top of the pergola to filter the sunlight.

180. Outdoor living room in Long Beach, California. Recently created in the Craftsman style, this is a classic example of an outdoor room built to complement an adjoining 1911 shingled house at the right. Set apart from the rest of the garden, this area was raised up a few steps to allow views of the ocean. The room is defined by an overhead structure of beams arranged in a shallow peak to support vines like an oversize pergola. With a sloping copper hood and wide wooden mantel below a tapering chimney, the handsome brick fireplace is enhanced by massive andirons. Seating is provided by a built-in bench along the window wall and by various other brick-capped ledges close to the fireplace or at the stairs. A large suspended Craftsman-style lantern is the only visible part of a concealed lighting system. (For other views see figs. 109, 116.)

181. Pergola-covered entry courtyard in Solana Beach, California. Looking back toward the entry from the house, this view shows most features of a charming outdoor room that has the secluded feeling of a walled courtyard. It was created as part of a major renovation of a nondescript 1950s house in a desirable location. Craftsman style inspired the dramatically framed pergola above, while the terra-cotta pavers, white stucco walls, and clay-tile roofing are Spanish Colonial. This perfect plant display area readily changes with new acquisitions or seasonal blooms, and a fireplace along the left side of the room invites pulling up a seat or relaxing beneath the stars; only the nearby treetops are able to see inside. (For other views see figs. 132, 143, 271.)

Furnishing the Garden

Outdoor Furniture such as Benches, Swings, Chairs, Tables, and Built-in Seating

Along with the concept of bungalow gardens as being outdoor living areas there develops the need to consider the design of garden furniture. The issues concerning the selection of outdoor furniture are comparable to those for interiors—harmony with the setting and durability of materials should be prevailing considerations. No matter where it is used, furniture in the garden should never compete with or overwhelm the natural surroundings, but seek to appear as much a part of them as possible.

With their material and construction being more of the Industrial Revolution period than the Arts and Crafts Movement, examples of garden furniture made of heavy steel wire (fig. 191) are among the oldest surviving examples. The use of cast iron for mass-produced garden furniture usually had whimsical naturalistic forms (fig. 142), a Victorian-era conceit that is less at home in a bungalow garden.

While not necessarily a direct result of the Movement, examples of wooden furniture in the Rustic style, made of woven willow branches or constructed of irregular logs (fig. 182), are generally compatible in an Arts and Crafts-inspired garden scheme. A more architectural but equally robust expression of natural materials is demonstrated by the use of natural stone to create garden furnishings (figs. 196, 197, 198, 199).

With the exception of some built-in examples attached to buildings that are still intact or have been restored (figs. 188, 189), the elements and usage over the years have ravaged most original wooden garden furnishings. On occasion, surviving period pieces may be found that were always kept in a well-protected and covered area (fig. 191). To address individual needs, some free-standing furniture was originally custom-designed to incorporate built-in

storage needs, and many such period designs can be re-created (or adapted) by a contemporary craftsperson.

Although too fragile to remain in uncovered areas for long, wicker furniture was long a standard choice for porches, and its popularity extended from the Victorian era well into the twentieth century. Combining handmade character and natural material, wicker furniture was advocated by Gustav Stickley, who also sold simple-lined examples (described as "woven willow") as part of his recommended furnishings for the ideal "Craftsman home." The lightweight and rather refined character of wicker allowed its interchangeability between outdoor and indoor use. Often more durable than wicker but equally useful is garden furniture made of rattan and bamboo. A good choice for informal covered areas, its materials invariably suggest an Oriental influence (figs. 163, 173).

Many period outdoor-furniture designs utilized simple straight lines that lent themselves to a variety of seating applications (fig. 183). Sometimes the functions of arbor and bench seating were attractively combined to create a garden focal point (fig. 183, no. 1; 184). A variation of the same design could incorporate a swing instead of a fixed bench (fig. 183, no. 10; 186). One of the most popular outdoor seating forms of the period, the swing was an essential feature of many bungalow front porches, whether suspended from chains attached to the ceiling (fig. 170), or with a fixed base (figs. 190, 192). A period garden-chair design of enduring utility and appeal is the wooden-slatted Adirondack chair, an old garden and summer-resort standby that has been reinterpreted in countless variations (figs. 41, 193), and was usually painted.

Garden furniture made of durable natural wood can be virtually maintenance-free and also tends to blend best with garden surroundings (figs. 184, 185). The muted weathered finish of some designs can be enlivened by color accents of a different material such as ceramic tile insets (fig. 195). The longest-surviving furniture is made of moisture and rot-resistant wood such as redwood or cedar (figs. 193, 194). Also durable are examples made of dense and resilient tropical woods such as teak, whose eventual silvery gray color can be enhanced by surface-growing mosses and lichens (fig. 185). Many are reproduced today in styles that derive from sturdy English park furniture (fig. 187) that feels quite at home with Arts and Crafts design.

182. Rustic circular garden seat (1914). Illustrated in Eugene O. Murmann's *California Gardens*, this seat was one of several examples of the rustic style that incorporated irregular branches and small logs in their design. Derived from similar furniture and architectural detailing of the so-called Adirondack style, rustic furniture like this has a handcrafted appearance that is more whimsical and picturesque than simple and functional, and no two pieces were exactly alike. Encircled by a bench with a fringe-like skirt of twigs below the seat and a back of asymmetrical curves and angles, this tree has been made into a garden focal point.

DESIGNS for GARDEN FURNITURE

183. Catalog illustrations: "Designs for Garden Furniture" (1926). This wide variety of furniture forms was illustrated in a catalog of the Southern Pine Association of New Orleans, Louisiana, called *Beautifying the Home Grounds.* They are intended as simple models that could be easily adapted, and they could "be built with the aid of only a hammer and saw." Their proportions were geared for standard-sized lumber. Although by this date popularity of the Craftsman style had declined in favor of historic revival styles, its influence is still apparent in the slatted backs and straight lines of these examples. The Arts and Crafts-derived angularity of the high-back bench or settle of design number 3 could do double duty as a screen, or as a facing pair would create an intimate outdoor room. The overhanging top and slatted panels in the table design of number 8 are borrowed from furniture for the interior of a Craftsman house. An example of the public's increasing taste for novelty over simplicity in Twenties design is seen in the Spider Web seat of number 1, while the bench design of number 2 is decidedly Colonial Revival.

184. Arbor with built-in seats in Berkeley, California. This design simultaneously fulfills the functions of a gate, an arbor, and seating. To extend the life of the narrow wooden elements, this kind of garden structure was usually painted. Despite its venerable appearance, this and most examples in use today are reconstructions of earlier designs.

185. Garden bench in southern Rhode Island. The fretwork pattern in the back of this bench was inspired by the Chinoiserie taste in architecture and furniture that was so fashionable in eighteenth-century England, America, and Europe. Due to the weathering of the unpainted teak, a pleasing patina has been made on this recently made variation of the Colonial Revival style. (For other views see figs. 21, 22, 97, 121, 137.)

186, Rustic garden swing of a house in the Windsor Square district of Los Angeles, California. Although similar in form to the garden arch and swing that is number 10 in figure 183, this example shows how a complete change of character is achieved through the use of unpeeled logs and branches, and its handmade quality evokes an Arts and Crafts sensibility. (For other views see figs. 26, 27, 80, 245; also *The Bungalow*, figs. 169-172, and *Inside the Bungalow*, figs. 66, 219.)

187. Bench and arbor of a bungalow in Portland, Oregon. An uninviting and narrow space at the side of a bungalow in Laurelhurst Park was transformed into this appealing brick-paved shade garden. The form of the teak bench was derived from examples used in English public parks. Framed by a narrow arbor, the wall of old painted clapboard siding on a garage makes a pleasingly subtle backdrop for the hanging plants. (For another view see *Inside the Bungalow*, fig. 195.)

188. Built-in benches at the entrance to a bungalow near Seattle, Washington (c.1910). A deep shed-roof extends over the original terra-cotta paving to create a small version of a covered porch without columns. Used to lend emphasis to the front door and further define the space, small built-in benches extend a feeling of informality and welcome to this tiny bungalow in its densely wooded setting. A vivid red color highlights the benches, front door, and window sash in handsome contrast to the subdued natural color of the shingled walls and surrounding woodwork. In the background the original garage is also a charming survivor of the period.

189. Detail of a built-in bench that is part of a porte cochère in South Pasadena, California (c.1907). Because of its placement across the side of a porte cochère, this bench is less likely to have been used for seating than as a place to set packages or luggage. It is opposite a few steps that lead to the porch and front door of the house. It is easy to see why the striking clinker-brick and river-rock masonry seen here was sometimes described as Peanut-Brittle style. (For other views see figs. 171, 193, 243.)

190. Glider and "bedroom" chairs on the rear deck of Sconehenge, Plymouth, Massachusetts. The pair of dark blue-green chairs were recently handcrafted by the owner from a design by English Arts and Crafts architect C.F.A. Voysey, and reveal a sense of humor, for cut into the upper-front leading edges of their sides are facial profiles. Called "bedroom" chairs on 1896 drawings by Voysey, there is no evidence that they were ever put into production. The chairs have casters for easy mobility. The new platform glider at the left has a more conservative design. Reconstructed to its original 1910 design, this deck enjoys views over the wooded site where the remnants of a period landscaping scheme (including a sunken garden) await full restoration. (For another view see fig. 174.)

191. Wire garden benches in Los Angeles, California (c.1900). These durable benches of heavy-guage steel appear delicate but are actually rock-solid and kept steady by their weighty angle-iron bases. Vintage examples from France, these are similar to others that were made in England and America, but are uncommon finds today. Set in a charming brick-paved pergola hung with wisteria, they almost disappear against the lattice-wall and feel remarkably compatible with the Arts and Crafts-inspired atmosphere of this recently created garden. (For other views see figs. 70, 71, 118, 119, 123, 125, 199; also *The Bungalow*, figs. 36-41)

192. Old Hickory glider on the front porch of the Keyes bungalow in Altadena, California (c.1915). Gliders, the more stable version of the porch swing, are a "low-tech" variant of the platform rocker that was developed in the Victorian era. Allowing the gentle movement of rocking chairs, platform versions don't have the same tendency to creep across a room. Old Hickory furniture was produced in a wealth of seating forms that were used in bungalows and other domestic interiors of the Arts and Crafts period, where simple, straight lines and natural unpeeled logs and woven rattan backs and seats were popular. Sometimes associated with the Adirondack style, it is best described as one of its more refined relatives; although hand-assembled, it was production-line furniture. Still produced today, the newer or more-pristine vintage indoor examples are characterized by rounded, highly-polished log ends that contrast with the bark.

193. Seating area under a pergola in South Pasadena, California (c.1907). Set against the house at ground level, open vine-covered beamwork shelters this area. These variations of the ever-popular Adirondack chair have the wide arms that double as narrow side tables and the slightly fanned-out boards in their backs. At the right is a two-seat version of the chair. It is interesting to note that it was far less common for bungalows to have original outdoor living spaces like this overlooking their rear gardens than it was to have a front porch. (For other views see figs. 171, 189, 243.)

195. Picnic table and benches at Henry Weaver house in Santa Monica, California. Custom made for this location, this picnic table and benches demonstrate a greater refinement of materials and of proportion than is typically expected. Inlays in geometric arrangements of tile accent the tabletop and bench seats and relate to the band of handmade ceramic tiles in the concrete paving.

196. Stone slab table or bench in La Jolla, Callifornia. Part of a garden composition of different stones, this example is as much sculpture as it is furniture. Set against feathery Mexican bamboo, the table/bench is used as a garden accent and is not part of a larger sitting area. The layered design of the base, which is built of the same flagstone used for the top, suggests a fragment of primitive stone architecture. In the lawn in front of it are two flagstones that help anchor the table/bench to the setting. At the left, the rounded form and lighter color of a granite boulder is an impromptu extra seat.

197. Stone garden bench at the Chick house in Oakland, California (1914). This bench does double duty as a part of a stone retaining wall that borders a hillside pathway. It also serves to break up visually a continuous length of boulder-buttressed wall. This garden surrounds one of architect Bernard Maybeck's most beautiful surviving homes in the Oakland hills. (For another view see fig. 58.)

194. *(Opposite)* Chaise longue under a pergola in Los Angeles, California. Derived from the adjustable back of the so-called Morris chair, this chaise longue reinterprets a favorite outdoor-furniture form that was popularized by resorts and oceanliners in the early twentieth century. The interior lounge chair that inspired it, originally designed by Philip Webb and sold by Morris and Company for many years, was widely imitated and was adapted by others into outdoor reclining versions like this. Shaded by a pergola that supports a mature profusion of bougainvillea *(Bougainvillea speclabilis)* this wooden deck area expands a small interior sitting room with French doors.

198. Stone hillside bench at the C. Hart Merriam house in Marin County, California. In a seamless blend of architecture and nature, this arc-shaped bench was recently fashioned with skill and artistry with large chunks of stone to buttress the hillside site. This retreat area has been paved with enormous stones similar to those of the bench. At the right, water from a natural spring runs through the hollow of an old mossy log and drips into a square-cut stone basin.

(Overleaf) 199. Stone and brick garden bench at the Keyes bungalow in Altadena, California. Reached by stepping across a meandering stream lined by granite boulders and river rock, a curving paved path leads to a brick-capped bench. The bench is used to imply a subtle destination point that seems to be a continuation of the surrounding landscape. The bench and stream are recently added features of a well-restored 1911 home.

133

In the Greene and Greene Garden

Views of Gardens and Their Details from Six Greene and Greene Houses in California

In the history of the American Arts and Crafts Movement, the buildings of the early twentieth-century architectural firm of the brothers Charles Sumner Greene (1868–1957) and Henry Mather Greene (1870–1954) is legendary. To a great extent, their projects embody domestic ideals of indoor-outdoor living that are inextricably linked to the garden.

Like so many Californians, the Greenes came from another part of the country. Born in Cincinnati, Ohio, they grew up mostly in St. Louis, Missouri, were educated at the Massachusetts Institute of Technology, and began their professional careers in architecture in Boston. Their aging parents had relocated to Pasadena, California, and in 1893 the brothers decided to join them there. There they found that the local economy was more than able to support a growing architectural practice. Working for the most part in Southern California, the brothers began their rapid climb to the peak period of their joint careers. Developing an attention to detail that sometimes bordered on the obsessive, they would attract their best clients—with progressively higher building budgets—in the first decade after 1900.

Like most other architects of their time, they began their careers designing in the popular historic revival styles of the day, including Queen Anne, Colonial Revival, and Mission Revival. But the sophisticated designs that most exemplify their work are a distillation of influences: English Arts and Crafts and American Craftsman sources are often cited, and almost always included with these is the influence of Asia and especially Japan. Some traces of Chinese design, such as the gentle curve of the "cloud-lift" motif, can also be found in details of their buildings and in the remarkable furniture that was created for some of them. Part of the fascination of their work is that none of these labels tells the complete story, so it is best considered in its own category.

While most clients of Greene and Greene were financially well-off, if not really wealthy, they tended to prefer restraint and understatement. Some projects were rather modest because that was most appropriate for the client's needs, and not necessarily the result of a limited budget (see figs. 201, 202). Their clients also tended to have sophisticated taste and appreciation of progressive design.

Even if it was expensive, a design that featured simple natural materials and beautiful joinery was still perceived as an expression of modesty, and wasn't intended to compete with the streetside prestige and glamour of one's own European palace or Italian villa plopped down in the California landscape. For the few who could afford it, however, a Greene and Greene house had its own kind of inverse snob appeal. The Greenes soon attracted more work than they could comfortably handle, for each project, no matter what its size, was a time-consuming challenge. Although some architectural and interior details became standards in their repertoire, little or nothing was cut that would compromise the quality of the final result.

The Greenes' conviction about their work included as much about the careful relationship of their houses to the landscape as it did about the exterior form of the house or the rooms and furnishings in their remarkable interiors. Outdoor living spaces demanded their own vocabulary of fixtures and furnishings; then there were the myriad issues of design, materials, and workmanship to consider for each project. As much as the forms of their houses, the architects' sense of the inherent beauty of natural materials, coupled with an extraordinary attention to workmanship, aligns them with most of the aesthetic (if not all of the philosophic) tenets of the Arts and Crafts Movement.

Sometimes called the "ultimate bungalows," the core group of masterpieces that have earned the Greenes their greatest fame have a particularly well-developed connection to outdoor living and their gardens. These projects include the David B. Gamble house (1907–1909) in Pasadena, their best known and most completely preserved project, which is open to the public as a house museum (see figs. 204–208). The other most significant homes in this group are the Robert R. Blacker house (1907–1908) in Pasadena (see fig. 203), and the Charles M. Pratt house (1908–1909) in Ojai. The only Northern California project comparable to these examples is the William R. Thorsen house (1908–1910) in Berkeley (see figs. 209–213). Reinforced by their use of predominantly horizontal lines and the colors and textures of natural materials, their houses interacted thoroughly with their surrounding gardens, so carefully framed views and outdoor living spaces abound.

Before and during this period, a number of other projects were completed by the Greenes; while generally lesser-known and on a somewhat smaller scale than the "ultimate bungalow" group, each has its own distinction and significance. Of the examples included in the following illustrations, all but the Garfield house are in Pasadena. The James A. Culbertson house (1902; fig. 200); the Dr. Frances F. Rowland house (1904; fig. 201); the Mrs. James A. Garfield house (1904) in South Pasadena (fig. 202); the Duncan-Irwin house, first built as the Katherine M. Duncan house (c.1900), but remodeled by the Greenes for its next owner as the Theodore M. Irwin house (1906; figs. 214–218); and the William W. Spinks house (1909; figs. 219–225). Examples of Greene and Greene architecture and interiors have been included in the two previous books of this series: The Gamble house was featured in *The Bungalow*, figures 123-127, and both the Thorsen and Gamble houses were featured in *Inside the Bungalow*, figures 152-173).

The work of Greene and Greene achieved considerable national recognition and was widely published in books and periodicals, including Gustav Stickley's magazine, *The Craftsman*. However, their active career together ended shortly after their greatest houses were built, and officially by the early Twenties. Already working on separate projects before the firm was dissolved, it was Charles Greene who on his own and away from Pasadena would achieve the greatest artistic success.

Between 1911 and 1928, he designed the house and gardens of Green Gables, a country estate for the Fleishhacker family in Woodside, California, near San Francisco. Although grand in scale, Green Gables reflects the English Cottage style, and its gardens have formally organized elements interpreted with rustic-stone detailing. Still owned by the family and surviving in excellent condition, highlights of the hillside complex include an extensive outdoor terrace attached to the house, which overlooks a large lily pond reflecting a view of wooded mountains. A much larger water garden is placed on a level below and reached by a pair of stone stairways built on top of arched forms that recall a Roman aqueduct. Across a vast rectangular pond that is 500 feet long a similar arcade is dramatically reflected in the water. The remarkable complex of house and gardens at Green Gables is the largest in America to be designed by an Arts and Crafts architect.

On a smaller scale, but exceptionally successful in forging a strong connection between the building and its site, was the singular design Charles Greene created for the David L. James house in Carmel, California. Painted in watercolor by Charles Greene on a visit in 1909, the romantic medieval ruins of Tintagel Castle on England's Cornwall coast were a direct inspiration for the design of the James house. The house was designed in 1916, but due to a protracted construction schedule lengthened by the architect's insistent perfectionism, the family couldn't move in until 1922. Overlooking the Pacific, the house was designed to appear as if it had grown out of its spectacular cliffside setting. The house is built of rough-edged granite in mostly horizontal courses that respond to the contours of the landscape. The building's arches and red-tile roof also show a Spanish or Mediterranean influence that makes it feel especially appropriate for California. Its gardens are important to the house, and most of them have plantings that are either indigenous or compatible with the local climate.

Gold of Ophir Rose over Pergola, Southern California.

200. Postcard view: "Gold of Ophir Rose over Pergola, Southern California," part of the James A. Culbertson house in Pasadena, California (1902). This postcard showcased the *Gold of Ophir* rose, a popular climbing variety of the period. *Ophir* in the Bible means a land rich in gold. This is the first of the Greenes' projects that included an open-timbered pergola, which predates their preference for rounding the ends of such heavy timbers. Later nicknamed the Peanut-Brittle style, the combined use of clinker brick and river rock throughout this project was another first for the architects. In the March 1906 issue of *Good Housekeeping* Una Nixon Hopkins said that the house had "cost about $6000 to build, yet it serves admirably as a model for more expensive mansions, while its simplicity and the abundance of its pleasing ideas hold out many possibilities to the builder of the veriest cottage."

A California Home.

201. Postcard view: "A California Home," the Dr. Frances F. Rowland house, Pasadena, California (1904). With a seated dog adding a homey touch, the subtropical plantings of this idyllic California setting are typical of the postcard imagery that helped popularize both bungalows and the Golden State. Although it is typical of many other Craftsman bungalows, this was the first of only two designs by the Greenes that ran a peaked roof ridge across the home's narrow direction, thereby creating side-facing gables and the low porch roof overhang in front. The front pergola of this house was added after it was moved from its original location. A sleeker alternative to a projecting dormer, the squared opening in the roof created a recessed deck space that admitted light and air to the second floor stair hall.

2658 – Southern California Winter Home of Mrs. Jas A. Garfield at Pasadena.

202. Postcard view: "Southern California Winter Home of Mrs. Jas. A. Garfield at Pasadena" (1904). If they were sufficiently prominent citizens, the homeowner's name was sometimes included on such postcards. Here the owner's name was probably mentioned because of her prominent past: Lucretia Garfield had been the former First Lady to President James Abram Garfield (1831–1881), who had been assassinated. Correspondence between client and architects reveals that Mrs. Garfield was very involved in the planning stages of the house, which is now located in South Pasadena. The simple Craftsman-style details and plain shingled walls of the house are enriched by clinker-brick and river-rock masonry.

203. Postcard view: "Oak Knoll Residence, Pasadena, California" (1907). With its more than 12,000 square feet of living space, the Blacker house remains the largest of Greene and Greene's "ultimate bungalows," and their most extravagantly appointed and detailed example. With a building budget that exceeded $100,000, it was also their most expensive. It was built for a lumberman whose wife, Nellie, was the sister of Mrs. Thorsen of Berkeley, California, who had also married a lumberman. This view of the U-shape house shows steps at the left that lead from a large covered terrace. At the right, a railing-enclosed roof creates an open deck for the corner master bedroom. Through its dressing room is a rear sunroom at the left, whose angled glass doors lead to another roof deck that projects above a first-floor bedroom. The site's slope toward the left allows direct garden access from a basement billiard room located below this bedroom. There is a large covered terrace off the living room below the roof deck at the right. It is not surprising that as the subject of many widely circulated postcards the Blacker house attracted much attention. Although the extensive original landscaped grounds, which included the lake-size lily pond in the foreground, cannot be recovered, a recent, meticulous restoration of both the architecture and the interiors has returned dignity and most of its former glory to this great house.

14451

204. Garden gate of the David B. Gamble house, Pasadena, California (1908). The kitchen and other service areas of the house at the right are reached through this gate before going into a side yard and then to the rear garden areas. Resembling the skeleton of a small roof, an arbor structure of crossing timbers rises to a shallow peak above the gate and extends to either side over the fence in a ceremonial gesture that recalls some Japanese gateways. Oversized and irregular granite stepping stones gathered from the nearby Arroyo Seco are handsome counterpoints to the geometry of the gate.

205. Detail of the front steps at the Gamble house. Greene and Greene wanted nature to interact with their houses; here a mature creeping fig *(ficus pumila)* has long claimed its territory at the front steps and along the foundation walls of the house. The square terra-cotta pot was designed by the Greenes.

206. Lily pool at the rear terrace of the Gamble house. The meandering line of the low clinker-brick wall at the left defines the border of this splendid lily pool. The pierced wall allows an intriguing play of light and reflection amid the blooming water lilies *(Nymphaea odorata rosea)*. An elegant original copper and art-glass lantern raised on a square brick pier provides illumination and a vertical accent. Two sets of stairs connect the raised terrace areas with the lower lawn and garden.

207. Detail of a window box on the front of the Gamble house. The construction of this window box with its "finger-joint" detail secured by wooden pegs at either end is reminiscent of the architects' interior detailing and furniture designs. The distinctive rounded and stepped earthenware pot at the right was designed by the architects for the Gamble house; the same design has now been reproduced and is also used at the Thorsen house in Berkeley. (See figs. 209, 211).

208. Detail of the brick walkway at the lily pool of the Gamble house. In this stylization of natural forms, Greene and Greene achieved a relaxed elegance, for the brick paving with staggered edges achieves an irregular free-form effect, and it incorporates into its edges recessed boulders that seem a continuation of those in the pool. (For other views see figs. 204-207: also *The Bungalow*, figs. 123-127, and *Inside the Bungalow*, figs. 167-173.)

209. Front gateway of the William R. Thorsen house, Berkeley, California (1909). This gateway is one of two that lead to the clinker-brick stairways and the front door; set on massive square brick piers, each has a wrought iron arch that supports an original oversize copper lantern. While the front façade with its setback is allowed some planting area, the main garden space is behind the house. Close to the University of California campus, the Thorsen house has been owned since 1943 by the Sigma Phi Fraternity and is home to its Alpha of California chapter.

210. Detail of the front landing of the Thorsen house. This clinker-brick landing creates a richly colored and textured backdrop for the flowering cherry tree. Set into the front door, transom, and side windows are superb iridescent art-glass panels that depict the abstracted branches of a spreading tree.

211. Detail of the front façade at the Thorsen house. This view shows more of the dining room's projecting bay window at left and its "cloud-lift" motifs. Although it is massive, the clinker-brick stairway's graceful composition creates a visual platform that anchors the rest of the façade. Hidden by foliage, several discreet window openings in the clinker-brick foundation admit light to basement level rooms.

212. Garden gate of the Thorsen house. A surviving original feature, this unusual gate is supported on a simple pivot that is secured by projecting pins at the top and bottom ends of the square upright on the left side. Allowing access to the rear garden from the street, the gate is part of a fenced and covered breezeway that runs between the house at the right and the garage at the left. The horizontal lines of the surrounding fence create a striking frame for the gate's curving forms.

144

213. View from the rear covered terrace of the Thorsen house. A continuation of the gated breezeway that connects with the street, this covered terrace creates a sheltered, shady retreat overlooking the rear garden. At the right is the back of the living-room chimney. The columns have a tall post that is flanked by a pair of smaller side posts with top ends that are rounded and tapered to create an interesting profile. The iron straps that tie together the three-section posts are intended to be visually expressive as well as structurally functional, and are another favorite Greene and Greene detail. (For other views see figs. 209-212; also *Inside the Bungalow*, figs. 152-166.)

215. Retaining wall of the front terrace at the Duncan-Irwin house. Most of the tenacious vines on this fascinating wall were recently trimmed back the better to reveal the wonderfully irregular arrangement of boulders, river rock, and clinker brick. It is likely that Charles Greene supervised the careful placement of each piece. The line of the wall roughly follows the curving corner site; when seen from the street, it appears to float on a natural pedestal.

214. Corner benches at the front door of the Duncan-Irwin house. Reproduced from the architects' original drawings, these benches were designed and built for this spot, and they abut each other to provide a continuous seating unit. The straightforward construction and simple lines of the benches reflect the robust detailing of the house. At left is one of the art-glass sidelights flanking the front door.

(Overleaf) 216. View of the entry pergola at the Duncan-Irwin house, Pasadena, California (1906). What began as a small six-room house that was moved here from another location about 1900 for Katherine M. Duncan eventually became one of Greene and Greene's most fascinating projects when they remodeled the house in 1906 for Theodore M. Irwin. Among the additions made at that time was a completely new second-floor level that took advantage of the interesting spatial opportunity created by a small original central courtyard. The resulting house seems to ramble in and out of doors in a pleasantly confounding sequence of spaces. A recent restoration of this large entry pergola required the removal of most of the old, sculpturally sinuous wisteria covering it so that the structure is revealed. The entire project has excellent examples of the Greenes' familiar combination of clinker brick and river rock: the tapering columns and massive chimney at the left rise up almost as if organic. Marked by a peaked overhang, the front door is located within the recess at the left; the lanterns are original 1906 features.

218. Covered front terrace at the Duncan-Irwin house. The equivalent of a front porch, this covered front terrace is greatly expanded by an adjoining open terrace partly seen at the right that wraps around the house. Used as outdoor paving throughout are square terra-cotta tiles bordered with brick. The door on the far wall that was once used as the front door opens into a generous entry hall with a welcoming fireplace. In the revised arrangement the front door is now located off the pergola, and opens into the same room but from its opposite side. Well-detailed with through-tenons and wooden pegs, a series of angled trusses support the roof of the covered spaces. The upswept corners on the top of the original lantern were inspired by the roof of a pagoda.

217. (Opposite) Interior courtyard with lily pool at the Duncan-Irwin house. Epitomizing an ideal of indoor-outdoor living, this central courtyard space with light, air, and water liberates the heart of this house. It was a spatial feature of the original Katherine M. Duncan house that was incorporated into the Greenes' 1906 remodel for Theodore M. Irwin. Their addition of a full second floor created a unique opportunity to exploit the additional vertical space. They expanded it outward on the level above to include three sides of a circulation space bordered by railings (see the upper right) and a band of glass windows that let light into what was then a billiard room on the fourth side (see the upper left). All four walls of the rectangular courtyard open onto surrounding rooms; the doorway flanked by the two small windows leads to a vestibule area between the living and dining rooms. The dining room and kitchen areas are reached through the doors at the right. The raised circular lily pool is activated by gently splashing water that recirculates through hand-blown art glass apertures in the form of stylized lilies on curving stems. In the far corner is a towering *Ficus benjamina*.

219. Sleeping porch of the Spinks house. Tucked under the eaves, this sheltered space looks out beyond the garage roof at the left to the San Gabriel Mountains. Greene and Greene added sleeping porches to many of their houses. The iron straps seen around the beam above added structural strength. Because of the widespread belief in the early twentieth century that fresh air was a good tonic for respiratory ailments, sleeping porches were featured in many bungalow plans and became popular across the country. This fresh air craze also corresponded to a growing public interest in National Parks and outdoor camping as a leisure pastime.

220. Rear elevation and deck of the William W. Spinks house in Pasadena, California (1909). Built for a retired judge and his wife who had come to Pasadena from Victoria, British Columbia, this house is defined by its prominent roofline of a large single gable that faces front and back. The shingled walls rise a full two stories to a roomy attic used for a children's playroom and storage level in the gable peak. The Greenes provided a large raised wooden deck across the back of the house that adjoins the living and dining rooms. The present deck was reconstructed by the current owners according to the original drawings. Appearing to float above its cantilevered construction, the deck is supported by timbers that rest on a single large beam that runs lengthwise down the center of the deck. Rising at either end of the deck are two arbor structures recalling Japanese *torii*. The tree at the far left is a pomegranate *(Punica granatum)*.

221. Detail of the steps of the rear deck at the Spinks house. In a continuation of the deck's floating feeling, open risers are supported by a series of smaller telescoping beams that rest on a brick pad. This end of the deck shows the projecting end of the large central support beam that runs its length.

222. Rear hillside garden walk at the Spinks house. Most likely an original landscaping feature, this is one of a series of concrete-paved walkways and steps of serpentine form that descend the wooded hillside garden areas behind the house. Bordered with boulders and river rock at either side, the walks and steps are interrupted midway down the hill by a built-in bench. Vivid red-orange nasturtiums *(Tropaeolum majus)*, graced with a black cat at the left, thrive in this partly shaded area, where low-maintenance plants are favored. The fence at near right marks a corner of the vegetable garden enclosure.

151

223. Vegetable garden at the Spinks house. The enclosure
has been developed into a series of angular raised beds separated
by gravel pathways and stepping stones. Raised beds permit easy
maintenance and controlling plants like tomatoes and squash that
have large or rangy habits. The boards at the sides of these beds are
fitted together at their corners in a crossing detail that recalls the "fin-
ger-joints" seen in Greene and Greene's interiors and furniture. The
lemon tree at the left displays its bounty above the area's largest bed,
which contains young lettuces, Swiss chard, and peas growing up the
conical steel-cage support.

224. Brick path to the outdoor dining area at the Spinks house. This
space was recently developed to take advantage of an unused but
pleasantly sited area that was convenient to the house. This outdoor
room was created by Isabel Greene with an asymmetrical sequence of
rectangular brick pads set flush with the ground that serve as stepping
stones through a colorful mixed bed of flowering perennials. The
planting spaces between the brick pads allow for a graceful transition
between the lawn and garden.

225. View of the garage and vegetable-garden enclosure at the Spinks
house. The vegetable garden is neatly contained within its own
enclosure, as often found in many period garden plans like those illustrated earlier in this book. The current owners, who are avid gardeners, collaborated with Isabel Greene, a Santa Barbara landscape architect, who is a member of the Greene and Greene family. Although
compact, the area's exposure was well-situated for growing both vegetables and flowers. The area is defined by a restrained but rather
ceremonial gateway, whose form was derived from the pair of *torii*-
like arbor forms that appear on the rear deck of the house. In another
masterful touch that integrates new with old, the cross-bar of the gate
continues to the left and ties into the structure of the existing garage,
and open-lattice fencing encloses the garden. In the far corner next to
the garage is a lemon tree bearing many bright fruit. Outside the
enclosure there are roses and a variety of sun-loving perennials including different varieties of lavender.

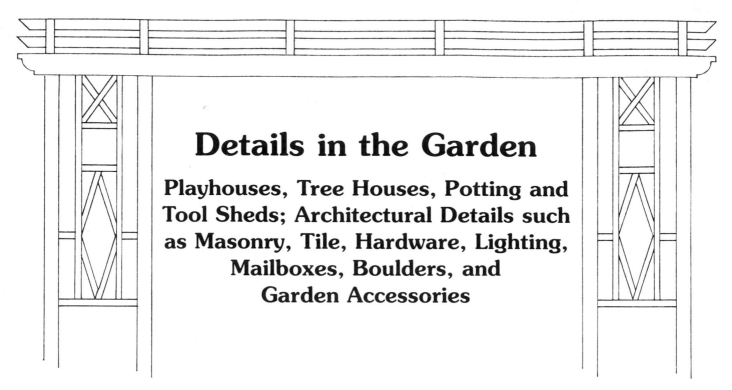

Details in the Garden

Playhouses, Tree Houses, Potting and Tool Sheds; Architectural Details such as Masonry, Tile, Hardware, Lighting, Mailboxes, Boulders, and Garden Accessories

A wealth of different categories has been combined in this chapter to create a visual idea bank of details for bungalow gardens, as well as related outdoor living and utility areas. These details constitute a helpful and illuminating reference that can guide those seeking to refine, upgrade, or restore their historic homes and gardens toward authentic (or sympathetic) Arts and Crafts-inspired design ideas and details that are sometimes missing. The details will also provide invaluable assistance to those who are planning or building houses the architecture of which interprets the Arts and Crafts style with entirely new construction.

Identified by date and description, original period examples have been included in each category whenever possible. Whether of the period or recently designed and crafted, most examples reflect the Arts and Crafts style, and a few other examples are included that reflect the diversity of bungalow architecture.

The range of details are arranged by the following categories and sequence:

(1) Architectural details:
  (a) children's playhouses and tree houses (figs. 226-229)
  (b) potting, tool and wood sheds (figs. 230-233)
  (c) storage and screen details (figs. 234-236)
  (d) trellis work and pergolas (figs. 237-240)
  (e) masonry and tile (figs. 241-246)
  (f) hardware (figs. 247-250)
(2) Lighting (figs. 251-265)
(3) Mailboxes (figs. 266-270)
(4) Boulders (figs. 271-274)
(5) Garden accessories (figs. 275-281)

226. Design for a children's playhouse (1934). Plans for this playhouse were offered for sale in *The Book of Lawn Furniture* published by the Long-Bell Lumber Company of Kansas City, Missouri, which included a materials list aimed at handy homeowners.

227. Children's playhouse in San Diego, California. A Craftsman-style bungalow in miniature, this accurately detailed shingled playhouse adorns the rear garden of a full-size 1910 house. Attention to detail shows in the exposed rafter tails, period light fixture, mailbox, children's picnic furniture, and small-scale container gardening. The interior could be used as a small study.

228. Children's playhouse in Pasadena, California. Set near the back of a rear garden, this playhouse adapts some of the details of its companion house, including the casement windows, clapboard siding, and Craftsman detailing. Embellished with river rock, it has been raised off the ground to create height for front steps and a small porch.

229. Children's tree house near Seattle, Washington. Built around two great fir trees, this shingled tree house is an A-frame construction. Always referred to as the "tree fort" by its current owners, the tree house was already in place when they moved here almost thirty years ago. In the background is a period garage (c.1915) built into the hillside.

230. Garden shed in Seattle, Washington. Limited side-yard space is well-utilized by this shallow but efficiently planned shed that holds a wealth of tools and garden supplies. With a shed roof and trellises on the sides, its design and materials harmonize with the new garden gate and fence at the right.

231. Potting shed in Seattle, Washington. Dubbed the "Potting Palace" by its owner, this side-yard shed is used for both gardening and entertaining needs. Its L-shaped plan allows generous counter space and room for a sink; there is also enclosed storage below and at the right. The steep roof pitch and heavy timbers are inspired by similar detailing at the house.

232. Garden shed in Wellesley, Massachusetts. Resembling a miniature house, this shed lends its comforting presence to a wooded garden. The cozy atmosphere is achieved by the exposed rafter tails, Craftsman-style lantern, Adirondack chair, raised landing, and plantings framing the entry. Although looking like a guesthouse, it functions purely as a commodious garden and household storage shed.

233. Wood storage shelter in Wellesley, Massachusetts. A narrow side yard area has been put to practical use by this covered shelter for a generous supply of firewood. The bracketing and rafter tails of the roof are Craftsman details repeated from the house.

234. Porch-column garden storage in Newton, Massachusetts. In an ingenious storage solution that is part of a recent remodeling, small gardening tools and supplies are kept handy on shelves concealed within the tapering thickness of a shingled front porch column. There is a second hollow column to hold taller tools. When closed, their shingled surfaces create an effective disguise for both.

235. Covered utility meter in San Diego, California. The necessary utility-service meters and surface-mounted power supply conduits can mar the lines of any house. On an outside corner behind this house, it was possible to conceal the units within a full-height enclosure with a screen-backed lattice door.

236. Wooden window grilles in Pacific Beach (San Diego), California. The flavor of an old California hacienda characterizes this remodeling. Against plain stucco walls irregular, rough wooden poles add rustic character throughout the project.

238. Detail of a climbing rose on a bungalow façade in Piedmont, California (1919). A favorite climbing rose of the period *(Cecile Brunner)* extends here an inviting gesture of warmth and charm to both visitors and passersby. Patience and diligent pruning are necessary, for based on the considerable thickness of its woody stem, this rose could date from the earliest years of the house.

237. Garage with wisteria at Ellsworth Storey houses in Seattle, Washington (1904). Highlighted against the dark aged wood, wisteria vines supported on trellis-extended eaves of this garage roof display their marvelous flowers. Original to the building, these sliding "barn" doors evoke the bungalow period far better than more contemporary doors.

239. Side yard arbor of bungalow in Portland, Oregon. Recent changes to this 1912 house included conversion of the former side driveway and rear garage into outdoor living space. Attached to an extension of the front porch, an arbor with some greenery spans the paved area. The new porch stair was made to match the existing concrete "stonework" seen on the chimney at the left.

240. Detail of an entry pergola in South Pasadena, California (c.1910). These original stylized classical columns at the corner of an entry pergola are entwined with wisteria and have a rough stucco finish that suggests age and character.

158

241. Detail of a front porch in San Diego, California (1912). Showcasing an unknown mason's artful style, this original clinkerbrick and river-rock foundation wall is accented with balanced patterns of smaller stones. At the center is a red-orange clivia *(Clivia miniata)* next to a deep pink camellia *(Camellia japonica)*. Nearly engulfed by the baby-tears *(Soleirolia soleirolii),* an edging of river rock echoes the rock work in the wall.

159

242. Detail of a brick planter wall at a patio in Pasadena, California (c.1910). This thick semicircular clinker-brick wall is filled with bright *Impatiens.* It echoes the two rounded bay windows of a study, which include a door leading to the small patio area.

243. Masonry detail in South Pasadena, California (c.1907). As exuberant as masonry of this period gets, this porch wall is full of movement, color, and texture. The undulating courses of clinker brick seem to be inspired by the motion of water as they dive over and under the bubble-like clusters of river rock.

244. Detail of a masonry column at Palisades Park, Santa Monica, California (c.1915). The front of this column has a simple brick frame for a decorative tile panel flanked with large rocks. Matte-glazed Batchelder tiles include the large central piece with stylized birds and grapevines surrounded by smaller tiles whose pattern was derived from ancient Byzantine textiles.

160

245. Detail of a gate post with brick and tile in the Windsor Square area of Los Angeles, California. This matte-glazed tile reproduces a classic Batchelder design of a vase of flowers that is highlighted by the subtle blue-gray color in the background.

246. Garden-wall tiles at Green Gates, Oakland, California (c.1923). This is one of two pairs of blackbird tiles that were set into the stucco walls that flank a garden niche. Manufactured by Calco (California Clay Products Company) of Los Angeles, they are notable for their vivid color, striking graphic design, and generous 16-inch height.

247. Detail of a copper downspout at the Henry Weaver house in Santa Monica, California (1911). The pointed ends of the copper support strap for the downspout are strikingly silhouetted by the limestone-color brick of the sloping foundation area of this house.

248. Copper garden-hose rack in Marin County, California. This hand-hammered copper garden accessory shows that even mundane functions can exhibit fine workmanship. Mounted to the wall by square-headed bolts, the rack's brackets are attached by round-headed rivets to a pair of backplates that have quadrants of pierced squares.

161

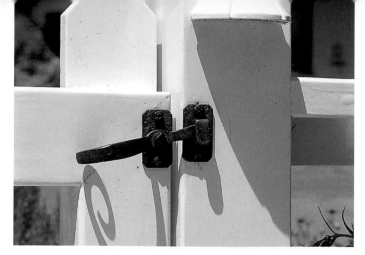

249. Iron garden gate latch in Marin County, California. Black iron has a timeless quality that feels at home in almost any period. The heartshaped forms used in this example recall a favorite motif used by English Arts and Crafts architect and designer C.F.A. Voysey in his hardware and furniture designs.

250. Iron garden-gate latch and post-mounted light in Marin County, California. Opening from the sidewalk, a low gate leading to the front path is opened by a turn of this simple latch. The spiral form of its gracefully curving handle is revealed by a midday shadow. Softly lighting up latch and gate at night, a downward-shining low-voltage light fixture is concealed in the half-conical shade on the post at the right.

251. Porch-ceiling light fixture of the Alexis Jean Fournier house in East Aurora, New York (c.1915). The spiraling lines of an original hand-blown glass shade set into a cylindrical wrought-iron frame decorated with curlicues are echoed on the suspension rod above in a flourish of delicately curled iron shaped like an elliptical spring. The decorative canopy should fit tightly to the ceiling. Adjoining the historic campus, this was the home of the well-known Roycroft painter.

252. Wall-mounted outdoor light at the Spinks house, Pasadena, California (1909). Although it is installed on a Greene and Greene house, this fixture was probably not designed by them. Its picturesque form has a storybook quaintness that is associated with English cottages, a strong influence on bungalows that appeared in some Arts and Crafts design. The fragile mica shade has a rich color.

253. Wall-mounted outdoor light fixture in Short Hills (Millburn), New Jersey (1907). The peaked form of this shade has pierced vent openings designed to release heat build-up from the light source. Glass panels once diffused light in its lower portion. The handcrafted form of this piece recalls old metalwork traditions of Colonial America and England.

254. Hanging outdoor lantern in Alameda, California (c.1910). Made of cast iron, the form of this period fixture is similar to many that are reproduced today. Resembling a small roof, the upsweep of its top makes the rectilinear form below more graceful. Looking like tiny dormer windows, the peaked forms on each of its four sides cover ventilation holes that release heat. The sides are shaded by stained glass (also sometimes called slag glass).

255. Wall-mounted outdoor lantern in San Diego, California (c.1910). This typical four-sided fixture has flat sides and a pyramidal top. Less typical is the monk's face seen on the backplate, which can also be found on numerous other forms of period fixtures (usually without the irreverently red-painted lips!).

256. Wall-mounted outdoor lantern in Alameda, California (c.1910). This large period copper fixture has refined detailing and good proportions. Small spade-shaped forms project around its top and also terminate the ends of each narrow strap that crosses over the slag glass. Recently mounted on a wood backplate, it hangs from a square beam topped with protective copper flashing.

257. Wall-mounted outdoor lantern at Craftsman Farms, Parsippany, New Jersey (1911). Exactly reproduced from an original Gustav Stickley design, this copper fixture is above an entrance doorway. The flared treatment of the bottom edge is similar to the lantern in figure 256, but the overall form of this example is less Japanesque and more traditional.

258. Hanging outdoor lantern with street numbers in Pasadena, California (1911). An original and still effective way to display a house number, this fixture has a slightly curved top with small peeled-back openings for heat release. The even color of its glass suggests a Japanese paper shade. In the background is a recently constructed fence with an adapted period design taken from an old photo of this property.

259. Hanging outdoor lantern in Alameda, California (c.1910). Unusual horizontal proportions give this lantern a compressed quality that is emphasized by its narrow glass openings with alternating green and amber slag-glass panels. It has a gray galvanized-metal finish that resembles lead. The lantern seems to exaggerate the scale of the meat hook from which it is suspended.

260. Wall-mounted outdoor light fixture at the Lanterman house in La Cañada Flintridge, California (1915). Easily mistaken for a modern design, this original period fixture has a Japanesque simplicity in the clean lines of its metal frame and white frosted glass shade. Mounted on unpainted stucco walls beneath a pergola that encircles much of the house, the fixture seems to confirm that the house had a progressive design for its day.

261. Wall-mounted outdoor light fixture in Pasadena, California (c.1925). This popular fixture was widely produced in many ways over the years. Its neo-traditional form blends well with many house styles. Protected by its wire cage, a thick ribbed-glass shade amplifies the light.

262. Column-mounted outdoor lantern in Wellesley, Massachusetts. Lighting a brick walkway down a narrow side yard, this recently crafted copper lantern is emphasized by being placed on top of a square column of irregularly stacked flat stones.

263. Outdoor lighting at an entry walk in Seattle, Washington (1909). The front walkway here needed lighting that would harmonize with the Craftsman-style house. Activated by a light-sensitive timer, the large lantern is set on a low brick-capped river-rock pedestal.

264. Hanging outdoor lantern in South Pasadena, California. Suspended from a knee-brace bracket beneath deep eaves, this copper and art-glass lantern was handcrafted by one of the current owners of this Craftsman-style home. In the style of the period, it adds harmonious color and design interest to a spot above French doors leading from the dining room to an outdoor living space in the garden.

265. Outdoor light and mailbox combination in Poway, California. Elevated on a sturdy wooden platform, an oversize mailbox has a letter slot in front and a cupboard door that opens to receive packages. On top is a Craftsman-style lantern with amber glass and large metal "roof."

266. Metal mailbox at Alexis Jean Fournier house in East Aurora, New York (c.1920). This example of factory-produced metalwork shows an Arts and Crafts influence. It is a typical form of the Twenties; many variations have been produced since.

267. Metal mailbox in Marin County, California (c.1920). This picturesque mailbox is another example of how Arts and Crafts design influenced machine-made products. The design of square rivets was impressed into the lift-up top and face, while the cast decorative shield with the gridded opening was made to look handcrafted.

268. Wooden mailbox in San Diego, California. Mounted on a porch column, this recently created design was made especially for this location. Its simple form incorporates such Craftsman-style elements as the pair of supporting brackets beneath the box and the series of square holes above a single vertical channel that reveal what mail may be inside.

269. Wooden mailbox in San Diego, California. Adding refinement to this new design is a pair of vintage metal hinges and a lock from an old box that were recycled as decorative elements. Able to accommodate generous amounts of mail, the design allows easy access through its horizontal form and wide slanted lid.

270. Bungalow-design mailbox in San Diego, California. The basic form of the bungalow in the background was the source of inspiration for the mailbox at the right. With good potential as a home project, many bungalow designs could be adapted for this purpose.

271. Front garden boulders in Solana Beach, California. Slightly below street grade, this front garden was designed more as a buffer to the street than as an outdoor-living area. Set around the lawn, light-color boulders glow amid the greenery, including palms and various flowers.

272. Front lawn boulders at the Henry Weaver house, Santa Monica, California (1911). The groups of boulders on the rolling lawn of this landmark bungalow set it apart from its neighbors. This reverence for the beauty of rocks is especially powerful in Japanese gardens. The lawn must always be neatly cut so that the rocks can be fully appreciated.

273. Planting bed with boulders in Pasadena, California. This front garden for a Craftsman house has a planting island surrounded by generous walkways of brick paving. Boulders are used to anchor the area along with low-maintenance shade plantings that incorporate a variety of colors and textures.

274. Detail of the planting bed with boulders in Pasadena, California. Here is another view of the flower bed shown in figure 273 showing the effective use of boulders to interrupt the brick edging. A mature tree that predated the creation of the planting bed became its dominant specimen.

276. "Turtle Garden" in Solana Beach, California. This homeowner has created an unusual and humane sanctuary for unwanted, sick, and abused turtles that are mostly cast-offs or returns retrieved from pet shops and animal shelters. The area has a low wooden enclosure and is landscaped to blend in with the surroundings. The reddish palm husk is a favorite, sheltered safety spot.

275. Garden bear at the Alexis Jean Fournier house, East Aurora, New York (c.1930). This cast-concrete bear is a relic of an era when animal-shaped lawn ornaments were popular as garden accessories. More common than bears were cast-concrete deer and ducks that were usually painted. Probably dating to the Thirties, the bear's mossy patina makes him seem much at home in an Arts and Crafts garden setting.

277. Birdhouse near Seattle, Washington. Handcrafted with a thatched roof, this artistically crafted birdhouse on a very tall post designed as a deterrent to prowling cats was recently added to this garden. Long a garden tradition, birdhouses can help activate gardens with song and activity of birds.

278. Butterfly house at the Roycroft Shops, East Aurora, New York. Set amid the blooms of a rhododendron, this narrow vertical structure was especially designed for the safe incubation of butterfly cocoons. An unusual garden accessory—and a good way for children to learn about nature—the house-like appearance gives it the same outward appeal as a birdhouse, but it is more suited to an eye-level spot.

279. Pedestal with a gazing ball at the Alexis Jean Fournier house, East Aurora, New York (c.1915). Also called a "witch's ball," silvered-glass globes were popular accents in early twentieth-century gardens and like concrete animals tended to be overused. They are still made today.

280. Sundial in South Pasadena, California. Recently created to complement a Craftsman-style house and garden, this cylindrical assembly of miscellaneous river rocks forms a rustic base for this sundial. Most period sundial faces were made of bronze and usually featured Roman numerals encircled by a wistful quotation concerning the passage of time or the beauty of a garden.

281. Sundial at the Alexis Jean Fournier house. East Aurora, New York (c.1920). Generally used as accent pieces rather than for telling time, sundials were one of the most popular garden accessories of the early twentieth century. This example has a low-relief depiction of Father Time on the bronze dial. The accompanying quotation is characteristic: "Grow old along with me, the best is yet to be."

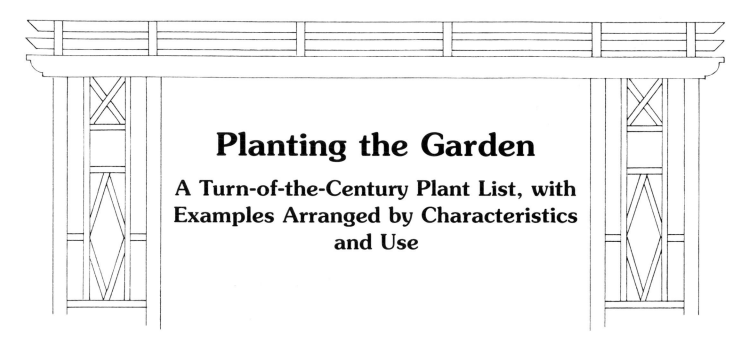

Planting the Garden

A Turn-of-the-Century Plant List, with Examples Arranged by Characteristics and Use

Gardening is one of America's consuming passions that generally eludes attachment to any specific era of our history. When looking back today at the practices and preferences of early twentieth-century gardening during the bungalow's heyday, they can be both a fascinating mirror of a time that seems so different, as well as a confirmation that perhaps things—at least in a garden— are remarkably unchanged. It is the timelessness of gardening that allows us to feel not only connected to the earth but also to our collective past.

The popularity of bungalows faded after 1930, a victim of the Great Depression and changing public tastes, but the national interest in home gardening that it helped to promote never waned. Sometimes the interest was more a necessity than a hobby; many Depression-era families used their vegetable gardens as significant food sources, and some annexed former flower beds for the same purpose. However, even in hard times, ornamental gardening remained a tremendously rewarding pastime. Gardening books and periodicals continued to be published, and many people found solace and comfort in their garden. The elbow-grease was free, and expenses for new garden

purchases could be minimized by trading plants and seeds with friends and neighbors. Almost without fail, diligent labors in the garden paid off with beautiful rewards.

Because many bungalow gardeners today are curious to learn more about what plantings were popular and most recommended for early twentieth-century gardens, the following plant list has been culled from a larger one that appeared in the appendix of a book called *How to Make a Flower Garden*, which was first published in 1901 by Doubleday, Page and Company. The copy from which this list is reproduced was a 1903 reprint, and it still bears a handwritten dedication in 1913 from the author's grandmother, Phoebe, to her husband, Dr. Clarence Duchscherer; both were lifelong gardening enthusiasts.

Please note that some of the common and botanical names for plants found in this list are different from how they are identified in more recent publications. Their currently accepted identities can be found by checking listings in a comprehensive plant encyclopedia or by consulting a certified nurseryman or other landscape professional. The abbreviation "spp." found after some of the plant names means "species."

EDITORIAL NOTE.—The following lists are believed to be fundamentally different from all other lists of similar appearance. The great fault with the extended lists found in some expensive works on gardening is that they contain too few lists and too many plants in each list. Moreover, the Latin names are often put first or used to the exclusion of the common names. The result is that such lists appal the beginner and are never used. Those which follow are designed to be of everyday practical service to beginner and expert. The writer has resolutely turned his back upon the impossible idea of absolute completeness, which has made the old lists so repellant and impractical. The keynote of the present endeavor is *suggestiveness*. Hence there are many lists and few plants in each list. This must be the right principle. Surely, the average person does not need fifty or a hundred plants for some one special purpose. Four may be enough; six should be ample; ten names will give plenty of choice.

The net result of the old-time extensive list is to impress the beginner with the immense number of plants in cultivation. But such an idea is worse than useless, because it discourages the beginner. According to the *Cyclopedia of American Horticulture*, there are nearly twenty-five thousand species of plants cultivated in America. But what is the use of laying emphasis on a mere cyclopedic fact of such a character? There is another idea which is much more important, *viz.*, the great diversity of human needs and purposes which are comprised under the one word "floriculture." Here are two hundred lists of plants, and each list represents a distinct idea. There are at least two hundred distinct purposes for which people cultivate plants. The differentiation of these purposes must have its educational value. It is to be hoped that the following lists will help the amateur gardener to clear up his ideas and determine what he really wants. The author has a wide acquaintance with plants, and there are very few in the following lists with which he is not personally acquainted. A good many duplicates will be found—*e.g.*, the pansy appears in several lists, but this is part of the original plan, for the best plants are relatively few in number, and is is better to suggest common and easily grown ones for the various purposes to which they are adapted than rare and costly plants of doubtful suitability.

ANNUALS

Ten of the most popular annuals
Balsam, *Impatiens Balsamina.*
China Aster, *Callistephus hortensis.*
Marigold, *Tagetes* spp.
Mignonette, *Reseda* spp.
Morning-glory, *Ipomæa purpurea.*
Nasturtium, *Tropæolum* spp.
Pansy, *Viola tricolor.*
Petunia, spp.
Poppy, *Papaver* spp.
Verbena, *Verbena* spp.

Ten annuals useful as cut flowers
Alyssum, Sweet, *Alyssum maritimum.*
Aster, *Callistephus hortensis.*
Baby's Breath, *Gypsophila elegans.*
Coreopsis spp.
Cosmos, *Cosmos* spp.
Daisy, Swan River, *Brachycome iberidifolia.*
Nasturtium, *Tropæolum* spp.
Pansy, *Viola tricolor.*
Pea, Sweet, *Lathyrus odoratus.*
Stock, Ten Weeks, *Matthiola incana*, var. *annua.*

Six fragrant-flowered annuals
Alyssum, Sweet, *Alyssum maritimum.*
Bartonia, *Mentzelia Lindleyi.*
Mignonette, *Reseda* spp.
Pea, Sweet, *Lathyrus odoratus.*
Stock, Ten Weeks, *Matthiola incana*, var. *annua.*
Sultan, Sweet, *Centaurea moschata.*

Six everlasting-flowered annuals
Catananche cærulea.
Gomphrena globosa.
Helichrysum bracteatum.
Helipterum roseum.
Polypteris Hookeriana.
Xeranthemum annuum.

Six annuals that bloom for eight weeks or longer
Ageratum, *Ageratum conyzoides.*
Clarkia, *Clarkia elegans.*
Morning-glory, *Ipomæa purpurea.*
Nasturtium, *Tropæolum* spp.
Petunia, *Petunia* spp.
Zinnia, *Zinnia* spp.

Six climbing annuals
Balloon-vine, *Cardiospermum Halicacabum.*
Bean, Hyacinth, *Dolichos Lablab.*
Cypress-vine, *Ipomæa Quamoclit.*
Hop, Japanese, *Humulus Japonicus*, var. *variegatus.*
Moonflower, *Ipomæa Bona-nox.*
Morning-glory, *Ipomæa purpurea.*

Six annuals with striking foliage
Castor-bean, *Ricinus communis.*
Corn, Japanese variegated, *Zea Mays*, var. *Japonicus.*

Hemp, Giant, *Cannabis sativa*, var. *gigantea.*
Hop, Japanese, *Humulus Japonicus*, var. *variegatus.*
Nicotiana alata.
Prince's-father, *Amaranetus hypochondriacus.*

Six annuals that re-sow themselves—likely to prove troublesome
Hop, Japanese, *Humulus Japonicus*, var. *variegatus.*
Morning-glory, *Ipomæa purpurea.*
Nicotiana alata.
Poppy, *Papaver* spp.
Rose Moss, *Portulacca grandiflora.*
Shell-flower, *Moluccella lavis.*

Six annuals for successional sowing
Alyssum, Sweet, *Alyssum maritimum.*
Baby's Breath, *Gypsophila elegans.*
Clarkia, *Clarkia elegans.*
Pea, Sweet, *Lathyrus odoratus.*
Poppy, California, *Eschscholzia Californica.*
Stock, Ten Weeks, *Matthiola incana*, var. *annua.*

Six annuals for sunny places
Amaranths, *Amarantus* spp.
Balsam, *Impatiens Balsamina.*
Bean, Hyacinth, *Dolichos Lablab.*
Gaillardia, *Gaillardia* spp.
Nasturtium, *Tropæolum* spp.
Rose Moss, *Portulacca grandiflora.*

Six annuals for shady places
Godetia, *Œnothera* spp.
Musk-plant, *Mimulus moschatus.*
Nemophila, *Nemophila* spp.
Pansy, *Viola tricolor.*
Tarweed, *Madia elegans.*
Torenia, *Torenia* spp.

Six annuals for rocky places
Baby's Breath, *Gypsophila elegans.*
Candytuft, *Iberis* spp.
Catchfly, *Silene* spp.
Clarkia, *Clarkia elegans.*
Nasturtium, *Tropæolum* spp.
Rose Moss, *Portulacca grandiflora.*

Six annuals for sandy soil
Clarkia, *Clarkia elegans.*
Cobæa scandens.
Godetia, *Œnothera* spp.
Nasturtium; *Tropæolum* spp.
Portulacca, *Portulacca grandiflora.*
Zinnia, *Zinnia elegans.*

Six annuals for heavy soil
Alyssum, Sweet, *Alyssum maritimum.*
Chrysanthemum, *Chrysanthemum coronaria*, etc.
Godetia, *Œnothera* spp.
Pea, Sweet, *Lathyrus odoratus.*
Petunia, *Petunia* spp.
Zinnia, *Zinnia elegans.*

Six annuals for very cold climates
Alyssum, Sweet, *Alyssum maritimum.*

Clarkia elegans.
Marigold, *Tagetes* spp.
Pansy, *Viola tricolor.*
Pea, Sweet, *Lathyrus odoratus.*
Stock, Ten Weeks, *Matthiola incana*, var. *annua.*

Six annuals for warm climates
Amaranths, *Amarantus* spp.
Balsam, *Impatiens Balsamina.*
Moonflower, *Ipomæa Bona-nox.*
Morning-glory, *Ipomæa purpurea.*
Nasturtium, *Tropæolum* spp.
Rose Moss, *Portulacca grandiflora.*

PERENNIALS

Ten of the most popular perennials
Anemone spp.
Columbine, *Aquilegia* spp.
Coneflower, *Rudbeckia* spp.
Hollyhock, *Althæa rosea.*
Iris spp.
Larkspur, *Delphinium formosum,*
Peony, *Pæonia* spp.
Phlox spp.
Poppy, *Papaver* spp.
Sunflower, *Helianthus* spp.

Ten perennials useful for cut flowers
Anemone Japonica.
Columbine, *Aquilegia* spp.
Daisy, Giant, *Pyrethrum uliginosum.*
Gaillardia aristata.
Gas-plant, *Dictamnus albus.*
Larkspur, *Delphinium formosum.*
Pinks, *Dianthus* spp.
Rocket, Sweet, *Hesperis matronalis.*
Snapdragon, *Antirrhinum majus.*
Sunflower, *Helianthus debilis.*

Six perennials with fragrant flowers
Gas-plant, *Dictamnus albus.*
Goldentuft, *Alyssum, saxatile*, var. *compactum.*
Ground Nut, *Apios tuberosa.*
Rock-cress, *Arabis albida.*
Rocket Sweet, *Hesperis matronalis.*
Scotch Pink, *Dianthus plumarius.*

Six perennials with everlasting flowers
Ammobium alatum.
Briza maxima (grass).
Bromus brizæformis (grass).
Cat's Ear, *Antennaria dioica.*
Helichrysum grandiflorum.
Statice incana.

Six perennials that will bloom the first season
Butterfly Pea, *Centrosema Virginiana.*
Chrysanthemum morifolium.
Gaillardia aristata.
Larkspur, *Delphinium formosum.*
Pink, *Dianthus* spp.
Snapdragon, *Antirrhinum majus.*

Some perennials that may be cut after

282. View of a flower garden at Sunnyside, Tarrytown, New York. On a rise of land overlooking the Hudson River, this large flower garden is on the grounds of the home of Washington Irving (1783–1859), the famous American author. Irving settled here in the late 1830s, and enjoyed his pastoral life, entertaining friends, and raising flowers, fruit, and vegetables, which he quipped cost him twice what they would in a store. Open to the public as part of the Sunnyside property, this is an active horticultural endeavor that demonstrates traditional gardening practices to visitors, and includes a kitchen garden for growing vegetables. With a handcrafted quality that is both decorative and functional, the teepee-shape plant support reflects an Arts and Crafts aesthetic. Made of long, narrow twigs that have been woven together like a basket, it is used to support and display a season's worth of flowering vines before removal for the winter. A rustic-log arbor to be seen in the background supports the woodier stems of climbing roses. Bright accents rising above lower plants are two perfect spheres of an ornamental onion *(Allium giganteum).* (For other views see figs. 3, 98, 283.)

283. Kitchen garden and gardener's cottage at Sunnyside, Tarrytown, New York. Set against a backdrop of natural wooded beauty, this open patch of earth will soon be filled in with the rapid growth of the new season. Overlooked by the bungalow-like gardener's cottage, this charmingly informal garden creates an ideal picture of self-sufficiency. The garden is just one area of Washington Irving's estate that is accessible to visitors, who are invited to come enjoy its atmosphere, absorb its history, and observe firsthand its seasonal gardening practices. (For other views see figs. 3, 98, 282.)

Poppy-Shirley   Delphinium   Carnation   Nicotiana Affinis

California Poppy   Petunia   Cosmos   Verbena

Snapdragon   Bachelor's Button   Zinnia   Strawflower

Marigold   Phlox Drummondi   Centaurea Imperialis   Aster

172

284. *(Opposite)* "A Page of Annual Flowers Which Anyone Can Grow" (1923). Sixteen of the most popular annuals in America during the period of the bungalow's greatest popularity makes a useful reference for those interested in cultivating period taste in today's flower gardens. Many of these plants continue to be favorites of amateur gardeners. This illustration and the accompanying commentary appeared in the 1923 edition of *The Home*, an annual supplement that was sent to subscribers of *Women's Weekly*.

(Top row, left to right) **Shirley Poppy** *(Papaver rhoeas):* "Sometimes known as the Silk or Ghost poppy, these satiny flowers range from delicate shades of rose, apricot, salmon pink and blush to glowing crimson, all with white centers." **Delphinium** *(Delphinium ajacis):* "Very effective in borders and planted amongst shrubs, they continue long in bloom; the graceful spikes are much valued for vases." **Carnation** *(Dianthus caryophyllus):* "Long prized as a hardy border flower; easily grown in beds or in pots; those raised from seed bloom more profusely than propagated ones and are therefore preferred." **Nicotiana Affinis** *(Nicotiana alata grandifloria):* "A gem for bedding; a most showy bloomer giving a continuous display of waxy white flowers right through summer and autumn."

(Second row, left to right) **California Poppy** *(Eschscholtzia californica):* "The state flower of California; a bright, free-flowering plant of low-spreading growth and finely cut silver foliage; pure shades of yellow orange and crimson and produced from early spring until frost." **Petunia** *(Petunia hybrida):* "For freedom of bloom, variety of color and effectiveness, these have no equal; with only a little care, they will produce their handsome, sweet-scented flowers throughout the summer." **Cosmos** *(Cosmos bipinnatus):* "One of the most showy and useful of garden plants, bushy and compact; the flowers are borne on long delicate stems similar to single dahlias, with foliage very finely cut." **Verbena** *(Verbena hortensis):* "Popular for beds, borders, mounds, vases, and window boxes; frequently used as an undergrowth to tall plants like lilies; showy, often fragrant flowers are borne in constant succession from June until frost."

(Third row, left to right) **Snapdragon** *(Antirrhinum majus):* "For gorgeous coloring, few flowers can match the new strains of very large size; on immense long spikes and very fragrant, well adapted for cut flowers; easily raised by seed." **Bachelor's Button** *(Centaurea cyanus):* "This is not a pretentious plant, but will always charm by its simple beauty. It reseeds itself and may be used for naturalizing purposes." **Zinnia** *(Zinnia elegans):* "These flowers are of enormous size, thickly set with velvety petals. Healthy, vigorous, branching freely, these plants make excellent material for groups or cutting." **Strawflower** *(Helichrysum bracteatum):* "A most satisfactory plant for winter bouquets, they are also good for summer cutting; if cut before fully open and hung upside down to dry, they will hold their color long after drying."

(Bottom row, left to right) **Marigold** *(Tagetes erecta):* "When many bedding plants are past their prime, they offer a wealth of color that is simply invaluable. These African varieties produce large blossoms on tall plants; the French *(Tagetes patula)* are smaller, but the colors and markings are elegantly striped and spotted." **Phlox** *(Phlox Drumondil):* "The showiest and most easily raised of all the annuals, producing a continuous supply of the most attractive flowers; all the tints of the rainbow are represented with stripes, veins, and eyes of contrasting shades." **Giant Sweet Sultan** *(Centaurea imperialis):* "Undoubtedly the finest of all Sweet Sultans for cut-flower purposes; the beautiful, sweet scented flowers are borne on long stems, and when cut will last for several days in good condition." **Aster** *(Callistephus chinensis):* "During the last of the summer and early fall the garden is usually a riot of reds and yellows, so the asters in their dainty and distinct colors as well as their many attractive forms are a pleasing contrast. The long stems make them desirable for cut flowers."

flowering for a second crop of bloom
Coneflower, *Rudbeckia triloba.*
Larkspur, *Delphinium formosum.*
Goldentuft, *Alyssum saxatile.*

Six climbing perennials
Butterfly Pea, *Centrosema Virginiana.*
Clematis Viorna, var. *coccinea.*
Dolichos Japonicus, *Pueraria Thunbergiana.*
Ground Nut, *Apios tuberosa.*
Hop, Common, *Humulus Lupulus.*
Perennial Pea, *Lathyrus latifolius.*

Six perennials that blossom longer than eight weeks
Coral Bells, *Heuchera sanguinea.*
Marguerite, Golden, *Anthemis tinctoria.*
Perennial Pea, *Lathyrus latifolius.*
Poppy, Iceland, *Papaver nudicaule.*
Poppy-mallow, *Callirhoë involucrata,* var. *lineariloba.*
Sunflower, *Helianthus multiflorus.*

Six perennials to remain undisturbed for years
Gas-plant, *Dictamnus albus.*
Iris spp.
Peony, *Pæonia* spp.
Phlox spp.
Perennial Pea, *Lathyrus latifolius.*
Yucca filamentosa, etc.

Six perennials to be renewed every year or two
Columbine, *Aquilegia cærulea.*
Coneflower, *Rudbeckia triloba.*
Daisy, English, *Bellis perennis.*
Hollyhock, *Althea rosea.*
Poppy, Iceland, *Papaver nudicaule.*
Snapdragon, *Antirrhinum majus.*

Six perennials likely to prove troublesome by spreading
Balm, Fragrant, *Monarda didyma.*
Candytuft, *Iberis sempervirens.*
Goldenrod, *Solidago rigida.*
Ground Nut, *Apios tuberosa.*
Poppy, Plume, *Bocconia cordata.*
Sacaline, *Polygonum Sachalinense.*

Six perennials for sunny places
Coneflower, *Rudbeckia hirta.*
Guillardia aristata.
Golden Marguerite, *Anthemis tinctoria.*
Poppy-mallow, *Callirhoë involucrata,* var. *lineariloba.*
Rock-cress, *Arabis albida.*
Sunflower, *Helianthus* spp.

Six perennials for shady places
Anemone Pennsylvanica.
Bluebells, *Mertensia pulmonarioides.*
Bugleweed, *Ajuga reptens.*
Helleborus niger.
Phlox divaricata.
Shooting Star, *Dodecatheon Meadia.*

Six perennials for cold climates
Goldentuft, *Alyssum saxatile.*
Lychnis alpina.
Moss Pink, *Phlox subulata.*
Poppy, Iceland, *Papaver nudicaule.*
Rocket, Sweet, *Hesperis matronalis.*
Saxifrage, *Saxifraga* spp.

Six perennials for warm climates
Chrysanthemum spp.
Coneflower, *Rudbeckia hirta.*
Dianthus spp.
Funkia spp.
Gunnera manicata.
Iris Japonica.

Six drought-resisting perennials
Baby's Breath, *Gypsophila paniculata.*
Coneflower, *Rudbeckia hirta.*
Inula grandiflora.
Sedum spp.
Sunflower, *Helianthus* spp.
Yucca filamentosa, etc.

Six perennials that bloom after a frost
Chrysanthemum spp.
Goldentuft, *Alyssum saxatile.*
Gaillardia aristata.
Goldenrod, *Solidago* spp.
Perennial Pea, *Lathyrus latifolius.*
Poppy, Iceland, *Papaver nudicaule.*

Six perennials for rocky places
Anemone blanda.
Bluebells, *Mertensia pulmonarioides.*
Columbine, *Aquilegia* spp.
Moss-pink, *Phlox subulata.*
Rock-cress, *Arabis albida.*
Sun Rose, *Helianthemum Chamæcistus.*

Six perennials for sandy soil
Blazing-star, *Liatris* spp.
Helichrysum arenarium.
Poppy-mallow, *Callirhoë involucrata,* var. *lineariloba.*
Sacaline, *Polygonum Sachalinense.*
Sunflower, *Helianthus* spp.
Sun-rose, *Helianthemum canadense.*

Six perennials for heavy soil
Columbine, *Aquilegia* spp.
Forget-me-not, *Myosotis palustris.*
Gas-plant, *Dictamnus albus.*
Larkspur, *Delphinium formosum.*
Peony, *Pæonia* spp.
Phlox spp.

Six perennials for moist or low ground
Balm, Fragrant, *Monarda didyma.*
Cardinal Flower, *Lobelia cardinalis.*
Funkia spp.
Iris lavigata.
Joe-Pye-weed, *Eupatorium purpureum.*
Ranunculus aquaticus.

Six perennials that re-sow themselves
Beard-tongue, *Pentstemon* spp.
Cardinal Flower, *Lobelia cardinalis.*
Clematis Viorna, var. *coccinea.*
Forget-me-not, *Myosotis palustris.*
Gas-plant, *Dictamnus albus.*
Snapdragon, *Antirrhinum majus.*

Six perennials with striking foliage
Adam's Needle, *Yucca filamentosa.*
Anemone Japonica.
Eulalia, *Miscanthus Sinensis,* var. *zebrinus.*
Funkia spp.
Giant Reed, *Arundo Donax.*
Poppy, Plume, *Bocconia cordata.*

Six perennials less than one foot high
Candytuft, *Iberis sempervirens.*
Daisy, English, *Bellis Perennis.*
Forget-me-not, *Myosotis palustris.*
Moss Pink, *Phlox subulata.*
Rock-cress, *Aubrietia deltoidea.*
Shooting-star, *Dodecatheon Meadia.*

Six perennials from one to two feet high
Achillea ptarmica.
Balm, Fragrant, *Monarda didyma.*
Columbine, *Aquilegia Canadensis.*
Funkia subcordata.
Lychnis Viscaria.
Poppy, Iceland, *Papaver nudicaule.*

Six perennials from two to three feet high
Bleeding-heart, *Dicentra* spp.
Canterbury-bell, *Campanula Medium.*
Cardinal Flower, *Lobelia cardinalis.*
Flame Flower, *Kniphofia aloides.*
Gas-plant, *Dictamnus albus.*
Peony, *Pæonia* spp.

Six perennials from three to four feet high
Adam's Needle, *Yucca filamentosa.*
Daisy, Giant, *Pyrethrum uliginosum.*
Larkspur, *Delphinium formosum.*
Poppy, Oriental, *Papaver orientale.*
Sunflower, *Helianthus multiflorus.*
Tree Peony, *Pæonia Moutan.*

Six perennials from four to six feet high
Coneflower, *Rudbeckia maxima.*

Hollyhock, *Althea rosea.*
Japanese Eulalia, *Miscanthus,* var. *variegatus.*
Joe-Pye-weed, *Eupatorium purpureum.*
Ravenna Grass, *Erianthus Ravennæ.*
Zebra Grass, *Miscanthus Sinensis,* var. *zebrinus.*

Six perennials taller than six feet
Bugbane, *Cimicifuga racemosa.*
Crambe cordifolia.
Grass, Giant Rye, *Elymus condensatus.*
Reed, Giant, *Arundo Donax.*
Sacaline, *Polyganum Sachalinense.*
Sunflower, *Helianthus orgyalis.*

Six white-flowered perennials
Achillea ptarmica.
Adam's Needle, *Yucca filamentosa.*
Astilbe Japonica.
Daisy, *Bellis perennis.*
Day Lily, *Funkia* spp.
Rock-cress, *Arabis albida.*

Six lilac, magenta and purple-flowered perennials
Beard-tongue, *Pentstemon* spp.
Blazing-star, *Liatris elegans.*
Gas-plant, *Dictamnus albus.*
Pink, Fringed, *Dianthus superbus.*
Rock-cress, *Aubrietia deltoidea.*
Shooting-star, *Dodecatheon Meadia.*

Six blue-flowered perennials
Anemone blanda.
Clematis Davidiana.
Columbine, Rocky Mountain, *Aquilegia cærulea.*
Forget-me-not, *Myosotis palustris.*
Iris lavigata.
Larkspur, *Delphinium formosum.*

Six yellow-flowered perennials
Columbine, *Aquilegia chrysantha.*
Coneflower, *Rudbeckia* spp.
Gaillardia aristata.
Goldentuft, *Alyssum saxatile,* var. *compactum.*
Poppy, Iceland, *Papaver nudicaule.*
Sunflower, *Helianthus* spp.

Six pink-flowered perennials
Bleeding-heart, *Dicentra* spp.
Hollyhock, *Althea rosea.*
Lychnis Viscaria, var. *splendens.*
Moss-pink, *Phlox subulata.*
Peony, *Pæonia* spp.
Pink, *Dianthus* spp.

Six red-flowered perennials
Anemone Japonica.
Balm, Fragrant, *Monarda didyma.*
Cardinal Flower, *Lobelia cardinalis.*
Clematis Viorna, var. *coccinea.*
Coral Bells, *Heuchera sanguinea.*
Peony, *Pæonia* spp.

Perennials with variegated flowers: Many cultivated varieties of such perennials as *Lychnis Viscaria, Phlox paniculata, Dianthus,* etc.

SHRUBS

Ten of the most popular shrubs
Barberry, *Berberis vulgaris.*
Currant, Golden, *Ribes aureum.*
Deutzia gracilis.
Hydrangea paniculata grandiflora.
Lilac, *Syringa vulgaris.*
Rhododendron Catawbiense.
Snowball, *Viburnum Opulus.*
Spiræa spp.
Syringa or Mock-orange, *Philadelphus coronarius.*
Weigela, *Diervilla Japonica.*

Ten shrubs with fragrant flowers
Alder, White, *Clethra alnifolia.*
Allspice, Carolina, *Calycanthus floridus.*
Amorpha, Fragrant, *Amorpha fruticosa,* var. *fragrans.*

285. Advertisement: "A Pretty Garden for a Dollar" (1913). Appearing among many small advertisements in the April 1913 issue of *House and Garden*, this eye-catching headline must have certainly hooked a good number of bungalow owners on a limited budget. It seems remarkable today that along with twenty-four packets of different popular flower seeds the sender's dollar also bought "an attractive garden plan ensuring color harmony" by return mail. The simple but handsome Craftsman-style garden gate in this drawing could be easily adapted for a garden of today.

286. Circular multi-bedded planting plan (1916). This geometrically formal garden plan was included with an article in the October 1916 issue of *The Garden Magazine* by Camille Hart Irvine of Gettysburg, Pennsylvania. She proposed that her plan could provide "flowers for the entire summer in a yard twenty feet square." Although the variations in planting selections duplicated her own garden's arrangement, each of the six "pie-shaped" wedges (formed by three separate beds apiece) could also represent six *separate* garden plans (that could *each* be carried out around the circle). In graduated sizes, eighteen separate planting beds comprise the plan, separated by two-foot strips of lawn (equal to the width of a lawn mower). A sundial was indicated for placement at the center. Irvine's instructions specified that "the beds must be made up in the fall and dug deep, with plenty of manure spaded in, and a little sand, if the loam is too heavy." Although the other flowers could vary, she advocated planting tulips in each bed ("six to ten inches apart and three inches deep, with a bit of sand in each hole"), starting with golden yellow (*Chrysolora*) toward the center, then scarlet (*Belle Alliance*) in the next tier, ending with flaming red and yellow mixed (*Kaiserkroon*) in the outside beds. Each bed was then to be sown with seeds of the indicated annuals that will re-sow themselves from year to year. She advocated lower-height plants toward the center, with taller ones in the outside beds to "help hide the fence" (although differing conditions might dictate otherwise; variations with other geometric shapes could also be adapted for this same concept). Because of the cold winters of her local climate, the tulip bulbs required that she cover each bed with a thick layer of manure and straw each fall, to be raked off in the spring. Other than this, there would be no expense for this garden after the first year, and the bulbs "will not have to be disturbed for eight or ten years." This garden is full of ideas worthy of reconsideration today.

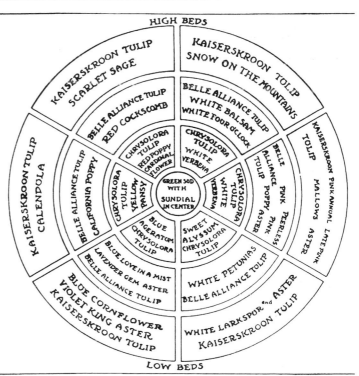

This plan of the beds shows how the combinations were graded by height

Currant, Golden, *Ribes aureum.*
Daphne Mezereum.
Elder, *Sambucus Canadensis.*
Lilac, *Syringa vulgaris.*
Mock-orange or Syringa, *Philadelphus coronarius.*
Oleaster, *Eleagnus argentea.*
Sheepberry, *Viburnum Lentago*

Ten shrubs whose individual flowers are large and showy
Azalea Calendulacea.
Azalea rhombica.
Carolina Allspice, *Calycanthus floridus.*
Magnolia Soulangiana.
Magnolia stellata.
Rhododendron Catawbiense.
Kerria, White, *Rhodotypos kerrioides.*
Rosa rugosa.
Rose of Sharon, *Hibiscus Syriacus.*
Stuartia pentagyna.

The shrubs which are completely covered with small but numerous flowers
Buckeye, Dwarf, *Æsculus parviflora.*
Buttonbush, *Cephalanthus occidentalis.*
Daphne Mezereum.
Exorchorda, *Exorchorda grandiflora.*
Fringe-tree, *Chionanthus Virginica.*
Judas-tree, *Cercis Canadensis.*
Quince, Japanese, *Cydonia Japonica.*
Smoke-tree, *Rhus Cotinus.*
Spicebush, *Lindera Benzoin.*
Thorn, *Cratægus Crus-galli.*

Six shrubs that blossom for eight or more weeks
Cinquefoil, Shrubby, *Potentilla fruticosa.*
Kerria, *Kerria Japonica.*
Pepperbush, Sweet, *Clethra alnifolia.*
Red Root, *Ceanothus Americanus.*
St. John's Wort, *Hypericum prolificum*
Staggerbush, *Pieris Mariana.*

Six shrubs useful for cut flowers
Almond, Double Flowering, *Prunus Japonica.*
Currant, Golden, *Ribes aureum.*
Deutzia gracilis.
Lilac, *Syringa vulgaris.*
Snowball, *Viburnum Opulus.*
Spiræa spp

Six shrubs attractive in fruit
Barberry, Thunberg's, *Berberis Thunbergii.*
Burning-bush, *Euonymus atropurpureus.*
Currant, Indian, *Symphoricarpus vulgaris.*
Kerria, White, *Rhodotypos kerrioides.*
Snowberry, *Symphoricarpus racemosus.*
Strawberry-bush, *Euonymus alatus.*

Six shrubs attractive in foliage
Allspice, Carolina, *Calycanthus floridus.*
Golden-bell, *Forsythia suspensa.*
Hydrangea, Oak-leaved, *Hydrangea quercifolia.*
Oleaster, *Elæagnus argentea.*
Raspberry, Flowering, *Rubus odoratus.*
Swallow Thorn, *Hippophaë rhamnoides.*

Six deciduous shrubs attractive during winter
Barberry, Thunberg's, *Berberis Thunbergii.*
Bramble, Japanese, *Rubus cratægifolius.*
Kerria, *Kerria Japonica.*
Kerria, White, *Rhodotypos kerrioides.*
Swallow Thorn, *Hippophaë rhamnoides.*
Winterberry, *Ilex verticellata.*

Six evergreen shrubs
Juniper, *Juniperus communis.*
Laurel, Mountain, *Kalmia latifolia.*
Mahonia, *Berberis Aquifolium.*
Pieris floribunda.
Pine, Dwarf, *Pinus pumila.*
Rhododendron Catawbiense.

Six shrubs attractive because of autumn colors with splendid foliage
Barberry, Thunberg's, *Berberis Thunbergii.*
Burning-bush, *Euonymus atropurpureus.*
Rose, Japanese, *Kerria Japonica.*
Strawberry-bush, *Euonymus alatus.*

Sumac, Dwarf, *Rhus copallina.*
Willow, Virginia, *Itea Virginica.*

Shrubs with variously colored foliage
Numerous horticultural varieties of many species, e. g.:
Purple-leaved Plum, Filbert and Barberry.
Golden-leaved Elderberry, Syringa and Hop-tree.
Variegated-leaved Althea, Weigela, Dogwood.

Shrubs to be protected from the winter sun
Certain evergreens with broad leaves, such as andromeda, mahonia, and some rhododendrons.
Planting on a northern exposure or in the shade of evergreens or even very branchy trees is generally effective.

Four shrubs with colored bark
Bailey's Osier, *Cornus Baileyi.*
Bramble, Japanese, *Rubus cratægifolius.*
Kerria, *Kerria Japonica.*
Strawberry-bush, *Euonymus Americanus.*

Four shrubs that resist drought
Cherry, Sand, *Prunus Bessyi.*
St. John's Wort, *Hypericum Kalmianum.*
Swallow Thorn, *Hippophaë rhamnoides.*
Tamarisk, *Tamarix Chinensis.*

Four shrubs likely to become troublesome by suckering, etc.
Cinquefoil, Shrubby, *Potentilla fruticosa.*
Ozier, Red-twigged, *Cornus stolonifera.*
Raspberry, Flowering, *Rubus odoratus.*
Swallow Thorn, *Hippophaë rhamnoides.*

Four shrubs for warm climates
Allspice, Carolina, *Calycanthus floridus.*
Camellia, American, *Stuartia pentagyna.*
Oleaster, *Elæagnus argentea.*
Weigela, *Diervilla* spp.

Four shrubs for cold climates
Buttonbush, *Cephalanthus occidentalis.*
Daphne Mezereum.
St. John's Wort, *Hypericum Kalmianum.*
Sheepberry, *Viburnum Lentago.*

Four shrubs suitable for sunny places
Allspice, Carolina, *Calycanthus floridus.*
Indigo, Bastard, *Amorpha fruticosa.*
Oleaster, *Elægnus argentea.*
Spiræa, Blue, *Caryopteris Mastacanthus.*

Four shrubs suitable for shady places
Andromeda floribunda.
Mahonia, *Berberis Aquifolium.*
Laurel, Mountain, *Kalmia latifolia.*
St. John's Wort, *Hypericum aureum.*

Four shrubs suitable for heavy soil
Cinquefoil, Shrubby, *Potentilla fruticosa.*
Lilac, *Syringa vulgaris.*
Rose of Sharon, *Hibiscus Syriacus.*
Thorn, *Cratægus Crus-galli.*

Four shrubs suitable for light soil
Bearberry, Red, *Arctostaphylos Uva-Ursi.*
Cherry, Sand, *Prunus pumila.*
St. Andrew's Cross, *Ascyrum hypericoides.*
St. John's Wort, *Hypericum prolificum.*

Four shrubs suitable for rocky places
Barberry, Creeping, *Berberis repens.*
Bearberry, Red, *Arctostaphylos Uva-Ursi.*
Crowberry, *Empetrum nigrum.*
Sweet Fern, *Comptonia asplenifolia.*

Four shrubs suitable for moist soil
Alder, White, *Clethra alnifolia.*
Holly, Mountain, *Nemopanthus fascicularis.*
Spicebush, *Benzoin odoriferum.*
Willow, Virginian, *Itea Virginica.*

Ten of the most popular hedge plants
Arbor-vitæ, American, *Thuya occidentalis.*
Hemlock, *Tsuga Canadensis.*
Holly, *Ilex crenata*, var. *microphylla.*
Honeysuckle, Tartarian, *Lonicera Tatarica.*
Locust, Honey, *Gleditschia triacanthos.*
Osage Orange, *Maclura aurantiaca.*
Privet, California, *Ligustrum ovaliflorum.*

Quince, Japanese, *Cydonia Japonica.*
Spruce, Norway, *Picea excelsa.*
Thorn, Cockspur, *Cratægus Crus-galli.*

Four evergreen hedge plants
Arbor-vitæ, American, *Thuya occidentalis.*
Hemlock, *Tsuga Canadensis.*
Holly, *Ilex crenata*, var. *microphylla.*
Spruce, Norway, *Picea excelsa.*

Four flowering hedge plants
Barberry, Thunberg's, *Berberis Thunbergii.*
Deutzia gracilis.
Quince, Japanese, *Cydonia Japonica.*
Spiræa prunifolia.

Four deciduous hedge plants
Buckthorn, *Rhamnus cathartica.*
Honeysuckle, Tartarian, *Lonicera Tatarica.*
Lilac, *Syringa vulgaris.*
Thorn, Cockspur, *Cratægus Crus-galli.*

TREES

Ten of the most popular trees
Basswood, *Gilia Americana.*
Buttonwood, *Platanus occidentalis.*
Chestnut, *Castanea Americana.*
Horse-chestnut, *Æsculus Hippocastanum.*
Locust, *Robinia Pseudacacia.*
Locust, Honey, *Gleditschia triacanthos.*
Maple, Sugar, *Acer sacharum.*
Pine, White, *Pinus strobus.*
Spruce, Norway, *Picea excelsa.*

Six trees with ornamental foliage
Angelica-tree, Chinese, *Aralia Chinensis.*
Catalpa speciosa.
Coffee-tree, Kentucky, *Gymnocladus Canadensis.*
Cucumber-tree, Large-leaved, *Magnolia macrophylla.*
Locust, Honey, *Gleditschia triacanthos.*
Papaw, *Asimina triloba.*

Six trees with fragrant flowers
Linden, American, *Tilia Americana.*
Locust, Black, *Robinia Pseudacacia.*
Magnolia, *Yulan.*
Magnolia, *Hypoleuca.*
Pterostyrax hispida.
Yellow-wood, *Cladrastis tinctoria.*

Six trees with large individual flowers
Dogwood, Flowering, *Cornus Florida.*
Gordonia pubescens (not fully hardy).
Magnolia, *Hypoleuca.*
Magnolia, *Yulan.*
Papaw, American, *Asimina triloba.*
Tulip-tree, *Liriodendron Tulipifera.*

Six trees covered with small but numerous flowers
Catalpa speciosa.
Goldenchain, *Laburnum vulgare.*
Laurel, Great, *Rhododendron maximum.*
Lilac, Japanese, *Syringa Japonica.*
Maple, Red, *Acer rubrum.*
Yellow-wood, *Cladrastis tinctoria.*

Six trees with attractive autumn foliage
Maple, Sugar, *Acer sacharum.*
Oak, White, *Quercus alba.*
Pepperidge, *Nyssa sylvatica.*
Sassafras, *Sassafras officinale.*
Sweet-gum, *Liquidambar styraciflua.*
Tulip-tree, *Liriodendron Tulipifera.*

Four evergreen trees
Holly, American, *Ilex opaca.*
Laurel, Giant, *Rhododendron maximum.*
Pine, White, *Pinus strobus.*
Spruce, Norway, *Picea excelsa.*

Four deciduous trees, attractive during winter
Birch, Paper, *Betula papyrifera.*
Pagoda-tree, Japanese, *Sophora Japonica.*
Sumac, Staghorn, *Rhus typhina.*
Willow, Yellow, *Salix Vitellina.*

Four trees with showy fruits
Cucumber-tree, Large-leaved, *Magnolia macrophylla*.
Holly, American, *Ilex opaca*.
Mountain Ash, American, *Sorbus Americana*.
Sumac, Staghorn, *Rhus typhina*.

Six trees suitable for city planting
Ash, American, *Fraxinus Americana*.
Buttonwood, *Platanus occidentalis*.
Locust, Honey, *Gleditschia triacanthos*.
Maidenhair-tree, *Ginkgo biloba*.
Pagoda-tree, Japanese, *Sophora Japonica*.
Tree of Heaven, *Ailanthus glandulosa* (pistillate).

Four trees suitable for seaside planting
Juniper, *Juniperus Virginica*.
Sassafras, *Sassafras officinalis*.
Spruce, White, *Picea alba*.
Tree of Heaven, *Ailanthus glandulosa* (pistillate).

Four weeping trees and trees with colored foliage
Horticultural varieties of numerous species, *e. g.*, Maple, Birch, Beech, Poplar, Oak, Willow, Elm, etc.

VINES

Ten of the most popular vines
Actinidia arguta.
Boston Ivy, *Ampelopsis tricuspidata*.
Clematis spp.
Cobæa scandens.
Dutchman's Pipe, *Aristolochia macrophylla*.
Honeysuckle, *Lonicera* spp.
Ivy, English, *Hedera Helix*.
Pea, Perennial, *Lathyrus latifolius*.
Trumpet-creeper, *Tecoma radicans*.
Wistaria Chinensis.

Six vines with showy flowers
Clematis spp.
Cobæa scandens.
Honeysuckle, *Lonicera* spp.
Moonflower, *Ipomæa Bona-nox*.
Pea, Perennial, *Lathyrus latifolius*.
Trumpet-creeper, *Tecoma radicans*.

Six vines with attractive foliage
Actinidia arguta.
Akebia quinata.
Boston Ivy, *Ampelopsis tricuspidata*.
Dutchman's Pipe, *Aristolochia macrophylla*.
Hop, Japanese, *Humulus Japonicus*, var. *variegatus*.
Silk Vine, *Periploca Græca*.

Six annual vines
Balloon-vine, *Cardiospermum Halicacabum*.
Bean, Scarlet Runner, *Phaseolus multiflorus*.
Canary-bird Flower, *Tropæolum peregrinum*.
Ipomæa versicolor.
Maurandia Barclaiana.
Thunbergia alata.

Six herbaceous perennial vines
Cinnamon-vine, *Dioscorea divaricata*.
Clematis, Scarlet, *Clematis Viorna*, var. *coccinea*.
Ground Nut, *Apios tuberosa*.
Hop, Common, *Humulus Lupulus*.
Pea, Butterfly, *Centrosema Virginiana*.
Pea, Perennial, *Lathyrus latifolius*.

Six vines with fragrant flowers
Actinidia polygama.
Akebia quinata.
Cinnamon-vine, *Dioscorea divaricata*.
Ground Nut, *Apios tuberosa*.
Honeysuckle, Hall's, *Lonicera Halliana*.
Silk-vine, *Periploca Græca*.

Six vines that bloom for more than four weeks
Clematis Viorna, var. *coccinea*.
Cobæa scandens.
Honeysuckle, Hall's, *Lonicera Halliana*.
Morning-glory, *Ipomæa purpurea*.
Pea, Perennial, *Lathyrus latifolius*.
Trumpet creeper, *Tecoma radicans*.

Six woody perennial vines
Akebia quinata.
Bitter-sweet, *Celastrus scandens*.
Matrimony Vine, *Lycium Chinense*.
Silk Vine, *Periploca Græca*.
Trumpet-creeper, *Tecoma radicans*.
Wistaria Chinensis.

FERNS

Six of the most popular hardy ferns
Christmas Fern, *Polystichum acrostichoides*.
Eagle Fern, *Pteris aquilina*.
Maidenhair, *Adiantum pedatum*.
Ostrich Fern, *Matteuccia Struthiopteris*.
Polypody, *Polypodium vulgare*.
Royal Fern, *Osmunda regalis*.

Four hardy ferns suitable for damp places
Marsh Fern, *Dryopteris Thelypteris*.
Royal Fern, *Osmunda regalis*.
Sensitive Fern, *Onoclea sensibilis*.
Wood Fern, *Dryopteris cristata*.

Four hardy ferns that will stand sunlight
Eagle Fern, *Pteris aquilina*.
New York Fern, *Dryopteris Noveboracense*.
Royal Fern, *Osmunda regalis*.
Sensitive Fern, *Onoclea sensibilis*.

Four hardy ferns that need shade
Chain Fern, *Woodwardia angustifolia*.
Lady Fern, *Felix-fæmina*.
Maidenhair, all spp.
Oak Fern, *Phegapteris Dryopteris*.

Four hardy ferns that succeed in partial shade
Cinnamon Fern, *Onoclea cinnamomea*.
Ebony Spleenwort, *Asplenium platyneuron*.
Purple-stemmed Cliff Brake, *Pellæa atropurpurea*.
Royal Fern, *Osmunda regalis*.

Four ferns suitable for dry places
Brittle Fern, *Cystopteris fragilis*.
Chain Fern, *Woodwardia Virginica*.
Polypody, *Polypodium vulgare*.
Purple-stemmed Cliff Brake, *Pellæa atropurpurea*.

Four evergreen ferns
Ebony Spleenwort, *Asplenium ebeneum*.
Grape Fern, Cut-leaved, *Botrychium dissectum*.
Hairy-lip Fern, *Cheilanthes vestitia*.
Polypody, *Polypodium vulgare*.

BULBS

Ten of the most popular hardy bulbs
Crocus spp.
Daffodil, *Narcissus Pseudo-Narcissus*.
Gladiolus spp.
Hyacinth, *Hyacinthus* spp.
Jonquil, *Narcissus Jonquilla*.
Lily, *Lilium* spp.
Narcissus, Poet's, *Narcissus poeticus*.
Tiger Flower, *Tigridia* spp.
Tulip, *Tulipa* spp.
Zephyr Flower, *Zephyranthes* spp.

Six of the most popular plants with tubers, rhizomes, etc.
Begonia, tuberous.
Canna spp.
Dahlia spp.
Elephant's Ear, *Colocasia antiquorum*, var. *esculentum*.
Lily-of-the-valley, *Convallaria majalis*.
Tuberose, *Polianthes tuberosa*.

AQUATIC AND BOG PLANTS

Ten of the most popular aquatics (excluding water-lilies)
Arrowhead, *Sagittaria* spp.
Arum, Water, *Calla* spp.
Cardinal Flower, *Lobelia cardinalis*.
Flag, Blue, *Iris* spp.
Floating-heart, *Limnanthemum lacunosum*.
Lotus, American, *Nelumbo* spp.
Pickerel-weed, *Pontederia* spp.
Swamp-pink, *Helonias bullata*.
Victoria spp.
Water-lily, *Nymphæa* spp.

Four aquatic plants for bogs and gardens
Cardinal Flower, *Lobelia cardinalis*.
Flag, Blue, *Iris versicolor*.
Pitcher Plant, California, *Darlingtonia Californica*.
Swamp-pink, *Helonias bullata*.

Four aquatics for ponds
Floating-heart, *Limnanthemum lacunosum*.
Lotus, American, *Nelumbo lutea*.
Pondweed, Cape, *Aponogeton distachyum*.
Water-lily, *Nymphæa odorata*, etc.

Four aquatics less than one foot above the pond surface
Arum, Water, *Calla palustris*.
Floating-heart, *Limnanthemum lacunosum*.
Pitcher Plant, California, *Darlingtonia Californica*.
Pondweed, Cape, *Aponogeton distachyum*.

Four aquatics from one to three feet high
Flag, Blue, *Iris versicolor*.
Pickerel-weed, *Pontederia cordata*.
Swamp-pink, *Helonias bullata*.
Turtlehead, *Chelone glabra*.

Four aquatics more than three feet high
Aster, Purple Stem, *Aster puniceus*.
Cat-tail, Broad-leafed, *Typha latifolia*.
Nundo, *Ligusticum actæifolium*.
Rice, Indian Water, *Zigania miliacea*.

Four aquatics likely to spread unduly
Arrowhead, *Sagittaria* spp.
Cat-tail, *Typha* spp.
Golden-club, *Orontium* spp.
Floating-heart, *Limnanthemum lacunosum*.

ALPINE PLANTS AND ROCK GARDENS

Ten of the most popular rock plants
Baby's Breath, *Gypsophila repens*.
Bluebells, *Campanula rotundifolia*.
Columbine, Common, *Aquilegia Canadensis*.
Daphne Cneorum.
Foxglove, *Digitalis purpurea*.
Gas-plant, *Dictamnus albus*.
Golden-tuft, *Alyssum saxatile*.
Moss-pink, *Phlox subulata*.
Poppy, Iceland, *Papaver nudicaule*.
Saxifraga crassifolia.

Four rock plants, annuals
Clarkia elegans.
Daisy, Swan River, *Brachycome iberidifolia*.
Gilia micrantha.
Linaria alpina.

Four rock plants, herbaceous perennials
Harebell, Carpathian, *Campanula carpatica*.
Lamp Flower, *Lychnis Alpina*.
Poppy, Alpine, *Papaver Alpinum*.
Rock-cress, *Aubrietia deltoidea*.

Four shrubby rock plants
Barberry, Creeping, *Berberis repens*.
Crowberry, *Empetrum nigrum*.
Daphne Cneorum.
Laurel, Mountain, *Kalmia latifolia*.

PLANTS FROM JAPAN

Comparatively few people can afford a Japanese garden, but no one need deprive himself of a "Japanese corner" or "Japanese border," in which the most interesting plants of Japan may be grown by themselves according to American floricultural methods. No equal area in the world furnishes so large a list of desirable ornamental plants as Japan.

Ten of the flowers most popular in Japan
Apricot, Japanese, *Prunus Mume.*
Cherry, *Prunus Pseudo-Cerasus.*
Chrysanthemum spp.
Iris, Japanese, *Iris lævigata.*
Lily, Japanese, *Lilium auratum.*
Maple (autumn leaves considered as "flowers").
Morning-glory, *Ipomæa* spp.
Peony, *Pæonia* spp.
Plum, Japanese, *Prunus triflora.*
Quince, Japanese, *Cydonia Japonica.*

Six shrubs from Japan
Aucuba Japonica.
Bamboo, *Bambusa pygmæa.*
Cherry, Flowering, *Prunus Pseudo-Cerasus.*
Fatsia Japonica (Japanese rice paper plant).
Ligustrum Japonicum.
Rhodotypos Kerrioides.

Twenty perennials from Japan suited for the hardy border
Anemone cernua.
Anemone Japonica.
Aralia cordata.
Aquilegia Buergeriana.
Aster Tataricus.
Astilbe Japonica.
Campanula punctata.
Dicentra spectabilis.
Epimedium macranthum.
Eulalia, *Miscanthus* spp.
Funkia spp.
Hemerocallis spp.
Iris lævigata.
Lily, Japanese, *Lilium auratum.*
Ophiopogon spp.
Peony, *Pæonia officinalis.*
Peony Tree, *Pæonia Moutan.*
Petasites Japonica, var. *gigantea.*
Sedum Siebaldii.
Thermopsis jabacea.

Six hardy bulbs from Japan
Black Lily, *Fritillaria Camschatcensis.*
Lilium speciosum.
Lily, Tiger, *Lilium tigrinum.*
Lycoris sanguinea.
Lycoris squamigera.
Narcissus Tazetta.

WILD GARDENS

Six choice wild flowers and ferns
These plants should not be taken from the wild even for garden purposes. If ordered from dealers, be sure they are nursery-grown, not collected.
All native orchids, especially Lady's-slippers, *Cypripedium* spp.
Arbutus, Trailing, *Epigæa repens.*
Fringed Gentian, *Gentiana crinita.*
Hartford Fern, *Lygodium palmatum.*
Laurel, Giant, *Rhododendron maximum.*
Walking Fern, *Camptosorus rhizophyllus.*

Six wild flowers of easy cultivation that bloom in early spring
Bloodroot, *Sanguinaria Canadensis.*
Everlasting, *Antennaria plantaginifolia.*
Hepatica triloba.
Squirrel Corn, *Dicentra Canadensis.*
Spring Beauty, *Claytonia Virginica.*
Wind-flower, *Anemone nemorosa.*

Six robust-growing plants of the class that the beginner should start with
Artichoke, Jerusalem, *Helianthus tuberosus.*
Elder, common, *Sambucus Canadensis.*
Joe-Pye-weed, *Eupatorium purpureum.*
Poppy, Plume, *Bocconia cordata.*
Rudbeckia laciniata.
Teasel, Fuller's, *Dipsacus fullonum.*

Six wild flowers that are easily grown from seed
Bloodroot, *Sanguinaria Canadensis.*
Cardinal Flower, *Lobelia cardinalis.*
Columbine, *Aquilegia Canadensis.*
Cone-flower, *Rudbeckia hirta.*
Aster, New England, *Aster Novæ Anglæ.*
Sunflower, Graceful, *Helianthus orgyalis.*

Six hardy exotic perennials that are easily raised from seed and are suitable for the wild garden
Aquilegia atropurpurea.
Larkspur, *Delphinium formosum.*
Poppy, Iceland, *Papaver nudicaule.*
Rock-cress, *Arabis albida.*
Rocket-cress, *Arabis albida.*
Rocket, Sweet, *Hesperis matronalis.*
Snapdragon, *Antirrhinum majus.*

Six wild flowers that will bloom in April or earlier
Anemone nemorosa (wild flower).
Everlasting, *Antennaria plantaginifolia.*
Spring Beauty, *Claytonia virginica.*
Hepatica triloba.
Sanguinaria Canadensis, bloodroot.
Squirrel Corn, *Dicentra Canadensis.*

Six wild flowers that bloom in May
Everlasting, *Antennaria plantaginifolia.*
Columbine, *Aquilegia Canadensis.*
Jack-in-the-Pulpit, *Arisæma triphyllum.*
Sweet-william, wild, *Phlox maculata.*
Wake Robin, *Trillium grandiflorum.*
Yellow Water Crowfoot, *Ranunculus multi fidus.*

Six wild flowers that bloom in June
Common Elder, *Sambucus Canadensis.*
Cone-flower, *Rudbeckia hirta.*
Fragrant Balm, *Monarda didyma.*
Great Solomon's Seal, *Polygonatum giganteum.*
Shooting-star, *Dodecatheon Meadia.*
Tall Buttercup, *Ranunculus acris.*

Six wild flowers that bloom in July
Adam's Needle, *Yucca filamentosa.*
Bouncing Bet, *Saponaria officinalis.*
Butterweed, *Erigeron Canadensis.*
Cone-flower, *Rudbeckia speciosa.*
Monkey-flower, *Mimulus tigrinus.*
Purple Cone-flower, *Echinacea purpurea.*
Virgin's Bower, *Clematis Virginiana.*

Six wild flowers that bloom in August
Buttonbush, *Cephalanthus occidentalis.*
Cone-flower, *Rudbeckia laciniata.*
Elecampane, *Inula Helenium.*
Fuller's Teasel, *Dipsacus fullonum.*
Great Lobelia, *Lobelia syphilitica.*
Joe-Pye-weed, *Eupatorium purpureum.*

Six wild flowers that bloom in September
Blazing-star, *Liatris squarrosa.*
Boneset, *Eupatorium perfoliatum.*
Cardinal Flower, *Lobelia cardinalis.*
Cone-flower, *Rudbeckia triloba.*
Poppy, Plume, *Bocconia cordata.*
Trumpet-creeper, *Tecoma radicans.*

Six wild flowers that bloom in October
Daisy Fleabane, *Erigeron strigosus.*
Golden Aster, *Chrysopsis graminifolia.*
Goldenrod, *Solidago* spp.
Starwort, *Aster* spp.
Sunflower, *Helianthus.*
Swamp-flower, *Helianthus angustifolius.*
Witch-hazel, *Hamamelis.*

Six attractive wild flowers, in bark, berries, etc., from November to spring
Celastrus scandens.
Laurel, Giant Holly, *Ilex. Rhododendron maximum.*
Red-branched Dogwood, *Cornus stolonifera.*
Spindle Tree, *Euonymus.*
Thorns, *Cratægus,* various red-fruited spp.

BIBLIOGRAPHY

Anderson, Timothy J.; Moore, Eudora M.; Winter, Robert W. (eds.). *California Design 1910*. Pasadena, California; California Design Publications, 1974. Reprint, Santa Barbara, California, and Salt Lake City, Utah: Peregrine Smith, Inc., 1980.

Bisgrove, Richard. *The Gardens of Gertrude Jekyll*. Boston, Massachusetts, Toronto, London: Little, Brown and Company Limited, 1992.

Bosley, Edward R.; Clark, Robert Judson; Makinson, Randell L. *Last of the Ultimate Bungalows: The William R. Thorsen House of Greene and Greene*. Pasadena, California: The Gamble House, USC, 1996 (exhibition catalog).

Braunton, Ernest. *The Garden Beautiful in California*. Los Angeles, California: Cultivator Publishing Company, 1915.

Clark, Robert Judson (ed.). *The Arts and Crafts Movement in America*. Princeton, New Jersey: Princeton University Press, 1972.

Comstock, William Phillips. *Bungalows, Camps and Mountain Houses*. New York, New York: W.T. Comstock Company, 1915 (revised from original edition of 1908). Reprint, Washington, D.C.: The American Institute of Architects Press, 1990.

Current, William R., and Current, Karen. *Greene & Greene: Architects in the Residential Style*. Fort Worth, Texas: Amon Carter Museum of Western Art, 1974.

Engstrand, Iris H.W., and Ward, Mary F. *Rancho Guajome: An Architectural Legacy Preserved*. San Diego, California: The San Diego Historical Society, 1995 (reprint of Fall issue of *The Journal of San Diego History*).

Festing, Sally. *Gertrude Jekyll*. London: Penguin Books Ltd., 1991.

Freudenheim, Leslie Mandelson, and Sussman, Elisabeth. *Building with Nature: Roots of the San Francisco Bay Region Tradition*. Santa Barbara, California, and Salt Lake City, Utah: Peregrine Smith, Inc., 1974.

Goode, Patrick; Jellicoe, Geoffrey; Jellicoe, Susan; Lancaster, Michael (eds.). *The Oxford Companion to Gardens*. New York: Oxford University Press, 1991.

Goss, Peter L., and Trapp, Kenneth R. *The Bungalow Lifestyle and the Arts & Crafts Movement in the Intermountain West*. Salt Lake City, Utah: Utah Museum of Fine Arts, University of Utah, 1995 (exhibition catalog).

Hitchmough, Wendy. *Arts and Crafts Gardens*. New York, New York: Rizzoli International Publications, Inc., 1998.

Jekyll, Gertrude. *Colour Schemes for the Flower Garden*. London: Country Life, 1914. Reprint, Boston, Massachusetts, and Toronto: Little, Brown and Company Limited, 1988.

Jekyll, Gertrude, and Weaver, Lawrence. *Gardens for Small Country Houses*. London: Country Life, 1912. Reprint (as *Arts and Crafts Gardens: Gardens for Small Country Houses*), Woodbridge, Suffolk, England: Antique Collector's Club Limited, 1997.

Jekyll, Gertrude. *Garden Ornament*. London: Country Life, 1918. Reprint, Woodbridge, Suffolk, England: Antique Collector's Club Limited, 1982.

Jekyll, Gertrude. *Some English Gardens*. London: Longmans, Green and Company, 1904. Reprint (as *Classic English Gardens*), London: Studio Editions Limited, 1995.

Jekyll, Gertrude. *The Gardener's Essential Gertrude Jekyll*. Boston, Massachusetts: David R. Godine, Publisher, Inc., 1986.

Kaplan, Wendy. *"The Art That Is Life": The Arts and Crafts Movement in America, 1875-1920*. Boston, Massachusetts: Little, Brown and Company, 1987.

Keeler, Charles Augustus. *The Simple Home*. San Francisco, California: P. Elder, 1904. Reprint, Santa Barbara, California, and Salt Lake City, Utah: Peregrine Smith, Inc., 1979.

MacCarthy, Fiona. *William Morris: A Life for Our Time*. New York, New York: Alfred A. Knopf, Inc., 1995.

MacPhail, Elizabeth C. *Kate Sessions: Pioneer Horticulturalist*. San Diego, California: The San Diego Historical Society, 1976.

Makinson, Randell L. *Greene and Greene: Architecture as Fine Art*. Salt Lake City, Utah: Gibbs M. Smith, Inc./Peregrine Smith Books, 1977.

_____. Greene & Greene: The Passion and the Legacy. Layton, Utah: Gibbs Smith, 1998.

McDonald, Elvin. *The 400 Best Garden Plants.* New York, New York: Random House, Inc., 1995.

Mitchell, Sydney B. *Gardening in California.* New York, New York: Doubleday, Page and Company, 1923.

Murmann, Eugene O. *California Gardens.* Los Angeles, California: Eugene O. Murmann, 1914.

Padilla, Victoria. *Southern California Gardens: An Illustrated History.* Santa Barbara, California: Allen A. Knoll, Publishers, 1994.

Parry, Linda (ed.). *William Morris.* London: Philip Wilson Publishers Limited, 1996. Reprint, New York, New York: Harry N. Abrams, Inc., 1996.

Pool, Mary Jane; Seebohm, Caroline (eds.). *House and Garden. 20th Century Decorating, Architecture, and Gardens.* New York, New York: Holt, Rinehart and Winston, 1980.

Saylor, Henry H. *Bungalows.* New York, New York: Robert M. McBride and Company, 1911.

Smith, Bruce, and Yamamoto, Yoshiko. *The Beautiful Necessity: Decorating With Arts and Crafts.* Layton, Utah: Gibbs Smith, Publisher, 1996.

Smith, Bruce (text) and Vertikoff, Alexander (photographs). *Greene & Greene Masterworks.* San Francisco, California: Chronicle Books, 1998.

Streatfield, David C. *California Gardens: Creating a New Eden.* New York, New York: Abbeville Press, 1994.

Stickley, Gustav. *The Best of Craftsman Homes.* Santa Barbara, California, and Salt Lake City, Utah: Peregrine Smith, Inc., 1979. (Includes plans from Stickley's *Craftsman Homes* (1909) and *More Craftsman Homes* (1912).

_____. *Craftsman Bungalows: 59 Homes from "The Craftsman".* Mineola, New York: Dover Publications, Inc., 1988. (This book reprints thirty-six articles selected from issues of *The Craftsman* magazine published between December 1903 and August 1916.)

Taylor, Norman (ed.). *The Garden Dictionary.* Boston, Massachusetts, and New York, New York: Houghton Mifflin Company, 1936.

Taylor, Patrick. *Period Gardens: New Life for Historic Landscapes.* New York, New York: Atlantic Monthly Press, 1991.

Trapp, Kenneth R. (ed.). *The Arts and Crafts Movement in California: Living the Good Life.* New York, New York: Abbeville Press Publishers, 1993.

Watkinson, Ray. *Willliam Morris as Designer.* London: Cassell Limited, 1967.

Winter, Robert. *The California Bungalow.* Los Angeles, California: Hennessey & Ingalls, Inc., 1980.

Woodbridge, Sally (ed.). *Bay Area Houses: New Edition.* Layton, Utah: Gibbs M. Smith, Inc., 1988.

Wright, Michael. *The Complete Handbook of Garden Plants.* New York, New York: Facts On File, 1984.

CREDITS

1. Miscellaneous credits

Fig. 61 is used courtesy Matthew Romanelli / Landscape Designer. Figs. 12, 14, 15, 135, 165, 202 are from the collection of Douglas Keister. Figs. 158, 284 are from the collection of Paul Duchscherer.

2. Archival-image credits

We are especially grateful to the following individuals for their generosity in sharing archival images from their private collections for use in this book: Figs. 73, 95, 183 are from the collection of Bob Elston. Figs. 11, 57, 160, 200, 201 are from the collection of Robert and Jackie Gustafson. Figs. 4, 10, 29. 72, 285, 286 are from the collection of Timothy Hansen and Dianne Ayres / Arts & Crafts Period Textiles. Fig. 203 is from the collection of Ed Herny. Figs. 13, 16, 23, 182 are from the collection of Gretchen Muller. Figs. 30, 93, 226 are from the collection of Robert Von Gunten.

3. General credits

Title page and figs. 77, 248, 249, 250: Fence and gate design and construction by Louis Yuvan; Lighting at spa by Ron Collier / Collier Lighting; Copper hose rack by Lowell Chaput, Metalsmith. Figs. 1, 67, 68, 69, 91, 268, 269: Designer: Michael Wheelden; Construction: Larry Word. Figs. 3, 98, 282, 283: Director of Horticulture / Historic Hudson Valley: Timothy Steinhoff; Landscape Manager for Westchester Properties: Mary Ann Witte; Sunnyside Site Director: Dina Rose Friedman. Fig. 5: Gardener: Joan Dukat. Figs. 21, 22, 97,121,137, 185: Courtesy Pauline C. Metcalf. Figs. 34-40, 49: Landscape Architect: Richard W. Fisher, ASLA / Toyon Design; Figs. 42-45: Landscape Architect: Keith R. Geller. Fig. 52: Landscape Architect: Nakano Dennis; Renovation Architect: Hoshide Williams / Robert L. Hoshide, principal architect; Project Architect: Grace Schlitt. Figs. 53-56, 155, 156, 198: Masonry for front steps: Tony Verondo; Design and labor for other areas: Julie Haas, Bill Pringle, and George Gonzales. Figs. 58, 197: Courtesy Foster Goldstrom. Fig. 59: Landscape Architect: Tom Bartos. Fig. 60: Landscape Architect (with owners): Richard W. Fisher, ASLA / Toyon Design. Fig. 62: Garden designed and installed by Matthew Romanelli / Landscape Designer. Figs. 64-66, 176: Landscape design by Arthur van der Beek / House of Orange, with John Zanakis. Figs. 74, 96, 234: Designed and built by John Tankard, Architect. Fig. 76: Renovation Architect: Joseph W. Greif. Fig. 79: Design and construction: Gerry Brown / Floating World Wood Design. Figs. 26, 27, 80, 186: Landcape and garden-furniture design by Scott D. Goldstein. Fig. 81: Designer: Donald Covington; Builder: Brian Klink. Fig. 82: Landscape Architect: Robert Trachtenberg; Gate design: Collaboration of Robert Trachtenberg and Jim Risley. Figs. 83, 128, 139, 170, 175: Landscape Architect: Ivy League Landscapes / Kelly A. Brignell and William L. Wilson; Restoration Contractor: Olde House Restoration Services / Mike Byrnes; General Contractor: Tom Champion Builders / Tom Champion; Landscape Contractor: Chinick Landscaping & Nursery, Inc. / Steve Chinick; Electrical Contractor: Heberle Electric / Jeff Heberle; Exterior paint: Benjamin Moore; Exterior paint / color scheme / design: Art First / Mary McMurray; Paint removal: Lyons Paint Removal / Mike Lyons; Painting Contractor (for house): Hytone Painting; Painting Contractor (for garden pavilion) Tom Kearcher; Masonry Contractor: R.L. McKee Masonry / Randy L. McKee; Reproduction of cast-concrete blocks: Vintage Block by Pacific Wholesale Supply / Greg Johnson; Cobblestone pavers: TerraCraft by Stone Products Corporation; Design and fabrication of fences, gates, arbor, trellises, raised garden beds by Decks Unlimited / Michael Jaeger; Custom screen doors by Truax Builders Supply, Inc.; Glazed terra-cotta pottery: Gladding McBean Co.; Gertrude Jekyll-designed urn reproduction from Wildwood Garden Furnishings; Lighting fixtures: Brass Light Gallery; Vintage porch swing from The Handwerk Shop / Brent and Linda Willis; Heirloom ("Sombrieul") roses from Heirloom Old Garden Roses. Fig. 84: Architect: Gary Sherquist; Construction: Michael Abrams. Fig. 85: Restoration by Elder Vides. Figs. 87, 151, 177, 236: Architect: James Galvin / Galvin+Cristilli Architects;

General Contractor: Beacham Construction Inc. Figs. 89, 126, 150: Designed by Kirk R. Thatcher. Figs. 90, 196: Architect: James Galvin / Galvin+Cristilli Architects; Collaborating designers: Louis and Debbie Beacham; General Contractor: Beacham Construction Inc. Fig. 92: Design and construction by Elder Vides. Fig. 100: Architect: The Johnson Partnership / Larry and Lani Johnson. Fig 102: Designer: Lynn Susholtz / Stone Paper Scissors. Fig. 103: Designer: Larry Kreisman. Figs. 122, 241: Garden design / construction: Larry Word. Fig. 127: General Contractor: R.B. Mohling Construction Company / Roger B. Mohling. Figs. 132, 181, 271: Architects / Landscape Architects: Adams Design Associates, Inc. / Stephen Adams; General Contractor: Brian Beeson Construction. Fig. 141: Landscape Architect: Nakano Dennis. Fig. 148: Garden design by Larry Kreisman; Tile by Tile Restoration Center / Marie Glasse Tapp / Delia Tapp; light fixture by Arroyo Craftsman. Figs. 152, 153: Pool design and construction by Aquatic Pools. Figs. 161, 260: Restoration by John Benriter. Figs. 163, 191: Landscape Architect: Thomas Batcheller Cox & Associates; Gardener: Reynaldo Cartagena. Fig. 172: Color scheme and painting by Elder Vides / Painting Concepts. Fig. 174: Folding screen, side chair and pedestal crafted by David Berman / Trustworth Studios. Fig. 178: Architects / Landscape Architects: Adams Design Associates, Inc. / Stephen Adams; General Contractor: Tekton Master Builders. Fig. 179: Architect: Daniel C. Lawrence; Construction: Elder Vides. Fig. 188: Landscape design / maintenance: Clifford Quality Landscapes. Fig. 190: Restoration of deck by David Berman; pair of Voysey-designed chairs reproduced by David Berman / Trustworth Studios. Fig. 195: Courtesy Lauren Rickey Greene. Figs. 223-225: Landscape Architect: Isabel Greene. Fig. 227: Designed and built by Bill Jones. Fig. 228: Designed and built by Michael Whalen. Fig. 230: Garden shed and walkway designed and built by Victor Munoz; gate and fence designed by Victor Munoz and built by Monicatti Building Contractors / Dennis Monicatti. Fig. 231: Designed by Gail Hongladarom / A Garden of Distinction; built by Lee Burnett. Figs. 232, 233: Designed and built by Tim McGinn. Fig. 245: Reproduction tile by Tile Restoration Center / Marie Glasse Tapp / Delia Tapp. Figs. 254, 256, 259: Period lighting courtesy of Arthur van der Beek and John Zanakis / The House of Orange. Figs. 7, 8, 257: Light fixtures reproduced by Ball & Ball. Fig. 258: Fence design and construction by Elder Vides. Fig. 261: Light fixture restored by Elder Vides. Fig. 262: Designed by Tim and Cindy McGinn; Masonry by Scott Southerland; light fixture by Arroyo Craftsman. Fig. 263: Architects: The Johnson Partnership; lighting fixtures by Arroyo Craftsman. Fig. 264: Light fixture designed and made by Frances Spradlin. Fig. 267: Designed and built by Roger B. Mohling / R.B. Mohling Construction Company. Fig. 270: Courtesy of Pat and Mike. Figs. 273, 274: Landscape design by Victor Lang.

A NOTE CONCERNING RESOURCES
AND HOW TO LOCATE THEM

There is an ever-increasing range of individual landscape architects and designers, as well as artisans, craftspeople, workshops, and other manufacturers who offer services or products with an Arts and Crafts sensibility across the country. Many sell their services or wares nationally, often by mail order, while others prefer to do business on a smaller scale or more local level.

While a number of the photographs in this book show the work of skilled landscape-design professionals, many are solely the result of the homeowner's own vision and hard work. Sometimes gardens represented are collaborative efforts of both. Because of space limitations, there are many fine examples of landscaping and garden-related work which was photographed but does not appear in these pages. Should the work of anyone that does appear here remain unidentified and uncredited, we apologize for any such unintentional omissions. The primary source for our crediting information was provided by the homeowners, and it is possible that some pertinent information remained incomplete at the time this book went to press.

Rather than attempt the impossible and assemble a definitive list of every noteworthy resource available today, we have instead opted to include a brief listing of periodicals which either specialize in or have regular coverage of Arts and Crafts-related design. While garden-related subjects are not a specific specialty of any of these magazines, all have included some in the past, and will likely continue to do so in the future. To encourage them, feedback from readers can be an effective tool, so let them know if you'd like to see more coverage of garden-related topics. While there are several excellent gardening periodicals in publication today, their emphasis (logically enough) is on plantings. For gardening ideas that are specific to historic styles or periods such as Arts and Crafts, and to housing forms such as bungalows, more specialized magazine resources are usually required.

Readers will find that many (if not most) of the Arts and Crafts resources that sell their wares nationally will be found as regular advertisers in the majority of the following periodicals. By consulting them routinely for such information, the likelihood of our readers receiving the most current names, addresses, and telephone numbers for such resources is ensured now, and in the future. To find various reputable resources that are specific to individual communities may require a bit of sleuthing; to this end, personal recommendations and referrals almost always work best.

American Bungalow
123 South Baldwin Avenue
P.O. Box 756
Sierra Madre, CA 91025-0756
(800) 350-3363

Style: 1900
17 South Main Street
Lambertville, NJ 08530
(609) 397-4104

Old House Interiors
2 Main Street
Gloucester, MA 01930
(800) 462-0211

Old House Journal
2 Main Street
Gloucester, MA 01930
(800) 234-3797

Traditional Building
69-A Seventh Avenue
Brooklyn, NY 11217
FAX: (718) 636-0750

The Tabby / The Arts & Crafts Press
P.O. Box 5217
Berkeley, CA 94705
(510) 595-1490

NOTE: Most of these periodicals also sell related books by mail.

The following is a fine source for books on the Arts and Crafts Movement, and its proceeds also help to support the ongoing maintenance of the Gamble House:

The Gamble House Bookstore
4 Westmoreland Place
Pasadena, CA 91003
(818) 449-4178

(Mail order catalog available by request)

For information regarding the Bungalow Heaven Landmark District, and its annual house tour, please contact:

Bungalow Heaven Neighborhood Association
P.O. Box 40672
Pasadena, CA 91114-7672
(818) 585-2172